Clergy Prayers
for Various Occasions

By Dr. D.L. Thomas, OSB

Incense From This Altar

Other books by D.L. Thomas:

Book of Common Prayer: In Modern English using the NASB

Training Teachers For Your Church

Then you will call upon Me and come and pray to Me, and I will listen to you. Jeremiah 29.12

Table of Contents

Priest's Prayers

The Making of Holy Water

Western Rite Making of Holy Water

(Priest wearing cassock, surplice, and stole)

Priest: Our help is in the name of the Lord.

Response: Who made heaven and earth.

Exorcism and Blessing of Salt (necessary for Exorcism of Water)
P: O salt, creature of God, I exorcise you by the living (+) God, by the true (+) God, by the holy (+) God, by the God who ordered you to be poured into the water by Elisha the prophet, so that its life-giving powers might be restored. I exorcise you so that you may become a means of salvation for believers, that you may bring health of soul and body to all who make use of you, and that you may put to flight and drive away from the places where you are sprinkled; every apparition, villainy, turn of devilish deceit, and every unclean spirit; adjured by him who will come to judge the living and the dead and the world by fire.

R: Amen.

P: Let us pray. Almighty and everlasting God, we humbly implore you, in your immeasurable kindness and love, to bless (+) this salt which you created and gave to the use of mankind, so that it may become a source of health for the minds and bodies of all who make use of it. May it rid whatever it touches or sprinkles of all uncleanness, and protect it from every assault of evil spirits. Through Christ our Lord.

R: Amen.

Exorcism and Blessing of Water
P: O water, creature of God, I exorcise you in the name of God the Father (+) Almighty, and in the name of Jesus (+) Christ His Son, our Lord, and in the power of the Holy (+) Spirit. I exorcise you so that you may put to flight all the power of the enemy, and be able to root out and supplant that enemy with his apostate angels, through the power of our Lord Jesus Christ, who will come to judge the living and the dead and the world by fire.

R: Amen.

P: Let us pray. O God, for the salvation of mankind, you built your greatest mysteries on this substance, water. In your kindness, hear our prayers and pour down the power of your blessing (+) into this element, made ready for many kinds of purifications. May this, your creature, become an agent of divine grace in the service of your mysteries, to drive away evil spirits and dispel sickness, so that everything in the homes and other buildings of the faithful that is sprinkled with this water, may be rid of all uncleanness and freed from every harm. Let no breath of infection and no disease-bearing air remain in these places. May the wiles of the lurking enemy prove of no avail. Let whatever might menace the safety and peace of those who live here be put to flight by the sprinkling of this water, so that the health obtained by calling upon your holy name, may be made secure against all attack. Through Christ our Lord.

R: Amen.

(Priest pours exorcised salt into the water, in the form of a cross)

P: May a mixture of salt and water now be made, in the name of the Father, and of the (+) Son, and of the Holy Spirit.

R: Amen.

P: The Lord be with you.

R: And with your spirit.

P: Let us pray. O God, Creator unconquerable, invincible King, Victor ever-glorious, you hold in check the forces bent on dominating us. You overcome the cruelty of the raging enemy, and in your power you beat down the wicked foe. Humbly and fearfully do we pray to you, O Lord, and we ask you to look with favor on this salt and water which you created. Shine on it with the light of your kindness. Sanctify it by the dew of your love, so that, through the invocation of your holy name, wherever this water and salt is sprinkled, it may turn aside every attack of the unclean spirit, and dispel the terrors of the poisonous serpent. And wherever we may be, make the Holy Spirit present to us, who now implore your mercy. Through Christ our Lord.

R: Amen.

Eastern Rite of Making Holy Water

Priest *(dressed in cassock and stole)*:

Blessed is our God always, both now and ever, and to the ages of ages. Amen.

Psalm 142

142 I cry out with my voice to the LORD;
With my voice I implore the LORD for compassion.
² I pour out my complaint before Him;

I declare my trouble before Him.
3 When my spirit felt weak within me,
You knew my path.
In the way where I walk
They have hidden a trap for me.
4 Look to the right and see;
For there is no one who regards me *favorably*;
There is no escape for me;
No one cares for my soul.
5 I cried out to You, LORD;
I said, "You are my refuge,
My portion in the land of the living.
6 Give *Your* attention to my cry,
For I have been brought very low;
Rescue me from my persecutors,
For they are too strong for me.
7 Bring my soul out of prison,
So that I may give thanks to Your name;
The righteous will surround me,
For You will look after me."

We then sing.

Tone 4

God is the Lord, and He has become manifest unto us; blessed is He who comes in the Name of the Lord.

Give thanks to the Lord and call upon His Name.

God is the Lord, and He has become manifest unto us; blessed is He who comes in the Name of the Lord.

All the nations encompassed me, and in the name of the Lord I crushed them.

God is the Lord, and He has become manifest unto us; blessed is He who comes in the Name of the Lord.

This was done by the Lord, and it is wonderful in our eyes.

God is the Lord, and He has become manifest unto us; blessed is He who comes in the Name of the Lord.

Troparia, Tone 4

To you, O Christ, we sinners now flee. In repentance we bow down before you, saying: "O Sovereign Lord, help us: have compassion on us, make haste to help, for we perish in the multitude of our sins Turn us not empty away, for we have you as our only hope.

Glory to the Father and to the Son and to the Holy Spirit, both now and ever and to the ages of ages. Amen.

Never, O Christ, will we, unworthy, cease to proclaim your powers: for if you did not hasten to our aid, making intercession, who would have delivered us from our manifold adversities? Who would have preserved us free to this day? We will not forsake you, O Lord Christ, for you save your servants from all malicious foes.

Psalm 51

[1]Be gracious to me, God, according to Your faithfulness;
According to the greatness of Your compassion, wipe out my wrongdoings.
[2] Wash me thoroughly from my guilt
And cleanse me from my sin.
[3] For I know my wrongdoings,
And my sin is constantly before me.
[4] Against You, You only, I have sinned

And done what is evil in Your sight,
So that You are justified when You speak
And blameless when You judge.
5 Behold, I was brought forth in guilt,
And in sin my mother conceived me.
6 Behold, You desire truth in the innermost being,
And in secret You will make wisdom known to me.
7 Purify me with hyssop, and I will be clean;
Cleanse me, and I will be whiter than snow.
8 Let me hear joy and gladness,
Let the bones You have broken rejoice.
9 Hide Your face from my sins
And wipe out all my guilty deeds.
10 Create in me a clean heart, God,
And renew a steadfast spirit within me.
11 Do not cast me away from Your presence,
And do not take Your Holy Spirit from me.
12 Restore to me the joy of Your salvation,
And sustain me with a willing spirit.
13 *Then* I will teach wrongdoers Your ways,
And sinners will be converted to You.
14 Save me from the guilt of bloodshed, God, the God of my salvation;
Then my tongue will joyfully sing of Your righteousness.
15 Lord, open my lips,
So that my mouth may declare Your praise.
16 For You do not delight in sacrifice, otherwise I would give it;
You do not take pleasure in burnt offering.
17 The sacrifices of God are a broken spirit;
A broken and a contrite heart, God, You will not despise.
18 By Your favor do good to Zion;
Build the walls of Jerusalem.
19 Then You will delight in righteous sacrifices,
In burnt offering and whole burnt offering;
Then bulls will be offered on Your altar.

We sing of your Holy Son, O God and cry aloud: from all adversities
save your servants, O Immortal One.

The praise of Kings, Prophets, Apostles, and Martyrs are you, and Intercessor of the world, O All-Powerful One.

I beseech You, O my Christ, give to me also, though unworthy, remission of offenses, I beseech You; through Your intercessions in that You are compassionate.

In you, O Christ, have I put my hope. Save me by your Cross; grant for me remission of sins.

All-praised Son of God, who through the Holy Spirit, in a manner beyond reason, became human, save our souls.

All-praised Sovereign Lord, we pray You: do not overlook the prayers of Your servants, so that we might be delivered from all tribulation.

From every sickness and infirmity. Deliver us, who have recourse unto you and your holy Protection.

O All-Holy Lord Christ, our Savior, save your servants from adversity and from all other necessity.

From every ban under which they labor deliver your servants from every ailment of body and spirit, O you most Holy.

Spare, O Savior, the souls of our brethren, who died in the Hope of Life; loose, and remit their sins.

Triadikon

We sing unto You, O God in Three Persons, crying aloud the thrice-Holy Hymn, entreating that we may receive salvation.

Priest:

Let us pray to the Lord.

People:

Lord have mercy.

Priest:

For Holy are You, O God, and to You are due all glory, honor, and adoration: to the Father and to the Son and to the Holy Spirit, both now and ever and to the ages of ages. Amen.

And the following

Troparia, Tone 8

Now draws nigh the time that sanctifies all men, and a just Judge awaits us; turn then, O my soul, to repentance, like the Adulteress tearfully crying: have mercy on me, O Lord.

O Christ, the Fountain, Who did sprinkle the waters of healing in the all-holy Temple of the Virgin, You, today, through the sprinkling of blessing did expel the maladies of ailing, O You Physician of our souls and bodies.

O All-Holy Lord Jesus Christ, guide aright the works of our hands, and entreat pardon for our transgressions, when we chant the angelic Hymn:

Holy God, Holy Mighty, Holy Immortal: have mercy on us. (3)

Glory to the Father and to the Son and to the Holy Spirit, both now and ever and to the ages of ages. Amen.

Holy God, Holy Mighty, Holy Immortal: have mercy on us.

Again

Holy God, Holy Mighty, Holy Immortal: have mercy on us.

Priest:

Let us be attentive.

The Prokeimenon, in Tone 4

The Lord is my Light and my Savior; whom then shall I fear? The Lord is the defender of my life; of whom then shall I be afraid?

Priest:

Wisdom! Let us be attentive! Let us hear the Holy Gospel.

Peace be to all. +

People:

And to your spirit.

Priest:

The Holy Gospel according to St. John. Let us attend.

People:

Glory to You, O God; Glory to You.

The Gospel

At that time, there was a feast of the Jews, and Jesus went up to Jerusalem. Now there is in Jerusalem by the Sheep Gate a pool, in Hebrew called Bethesda, which has five porticoes. In these lay a multitude of invalids, blind, lame, paralyzed, waiting for the moving of the water. For an angel of the Lord went down at certain seasons into the pool and troubled the water. And whoever stepped in first after the troubling of the water was healed of whatever disease he had.

Choir:

Glory to You, O God; Glory to You.

The Ektenia Of Blessing

Following each petition, the Choir responds with "Lord have mercy" and, at the end, with "To You, O Lord."

In peace let us pray to the Lord.

For the peace from above; for the salvation of our souls; let us pray to the Lord.

For the peace of the whole world; for the stability of the holy Churches of God; and for the union of all; let us pray to the Lord.

[For this holy House; and for them that with faith, reverence, and the fear of God enter therein; let us pray to the Lord.]

For our Bishop (Name), for all the Clergy, and the people, let us pray to the Lord.

[For the President of the United States and for all civil authorities; let us pray to the Lord.]

For this city, for every city and land, for the faithful that dwell in them, let us pray to the Lord.

For seasonable weather; for abundance of the fruits of the earth, and for peaceful seasons; let us pray to the Lord.

For all them that travel by land or sea, or in the air; for the sick, and the afflicted; for captives, and for their salvation; let us pray to the Lord.

That this water might be hallowed by the might, and operation, and descent of the Holy Spirit, let us pray to the Lord.

That there may descend upon these waters the cleansing operation of the super substantial Trinity; let us pray to the Lord.

That this water may be to the healing of souls and bodies, and to the banishment of every satanic and hostile power, let us pray to the Lord.

That there may be sent down upon it the Grace of Redemption, the blessing of the Jordan; let us pray to the Lord.

For all of them who need God to help and give protection, let us pray to the Lord.

That He will illuminate us with the Light of understanding of the Consubstantial Trinity; let us pray to the Lord.

That the Lord our God will show us forth as sons and daughters and heirs of His Kingdom through the partaking and sprinkling of these waters; let us pray to the Lord.

That He will deliver us from all tribulation, wrath, danger, and necessity, let us pray to the Lord.

Save, O Lord, Thy people and bless Thine inheritance, granting unto the faithful victory over enemies. And by the power of Thy Cross, do Thou preserve Thy Holy Church.

Help us; save us; have mercy on us; and keep us, O God, by Your Grace.

Calling to remembrance all the Saints, let us commend ourselves and one another and all our life to Christ our God.

People:

To You, O Lord.

Priest:

For to You do we send up all glory, honor, and worship: to the Father and to the Son and to the Holy Spirit, both now and ever, and to the ages of ages. Amen.

Let us pray to the Lord.

People:

Lord have mercy.

Priest:

O Lord our God, Who are mighty in counsel and wondrous in all Your deeds: the Creator of all things: Who keep Your Covenant and Your mercy upon all those who love You and keep Your commandments: Who receive the devout tears of all that are in distress: for this cause did You come in the similitude of a servant, scorning not our image but giving true health to the body and saying, "Lo! You are healed, sin no more." And with clay did make man's eyes whole, and having commanded him to wash, made him by Your word rejoice in the light, putting to confusion the floods of passions of enemies; and drying up the bitter sea of life of the same, subduing the waves of sensual desires heavy to be endured: do You, the same Lord and King Who loves mankind, Who has granted to us to clothe ourselves in the garment of snowy whiteness, by water and by Spirit: send down on us Your blessing, and through the partaking of this water, through sprinkling with it, wash away the defilement of passions.

Yea, we beseech You visit our weaknesses, O Good One, and heal our infirmities both of spirit and of body through Your mercy; through the mediation of the all-Holy, exceedingly blessed Lord Jesus Christ; Through the intercessions of the precious and life-creating Cross; through the protection of the glorious bodiless Powers of the Heavens; Preserve, Lord, the president of the United States, and all the other Civil Authorities enabled by the American people; save, O God, all orthodox Bishops who rightly divide the word of Your truth, granting unto them spiritual and bodily health; be merciful unto this Christian habitation which labors for You; have in remembrance, O God, every priestly and monastic order and their salvation; have in remembrance, O God, both those that hate us and those who love us, the brethren who serve with us; the people here present; and who for any cause are worthy of blessing and have gone forth having empowered us, unworthy though we are, to pray, for them; have in remembrance, O God, our brethren who are in captivity and affliction, and show mercy unto them according to Your great Mercy, delivering them from every tribulation.

For You are the Fountain of healing, O Christ our God, and to You do we send up all glory, together with Your Eternal Father and Your All-Holy, Good, and Life-creating Spirit, both now and ever, and to the ages of ages. Amen.

Peace be to all. (+)

People:

And to your spirit.

Priest:

Let us bow our heads before the Lord.

People:

To You, O Lord.

Priest: (inaudibly)

Bow down Your ear and listen to us, O Lord, Who deigned to be baptized in the river Jordan, and there sanctified the water. Bless us all who by the bowing of our heads do show forth our apprehension that we are Your servants. Grant that we may be filled with Your sanctification through the partaking of this water, and let it be for us, O Lord, for the health of soul and body.

(Aloud)

For You are the sanctification of our souls and bodies, and to You do we send up all glory: to the Father, and to the Son, and to the Holy Spirit, both now and ever, and to the ages of ages. Amen.

Then the Priest, taking up the venerable Cross, dips it crosswise in the Water thrice, singing the Troparion:

Tone 1

Save, O Lord, Your people, and bless Your inheritance, giving us victory over all who assail us and protecting the Church of Your faithful by Your Cross. (3)

Then the Priest sprinkles the Holy Water in the form of the Cross and sings:

Tone 2

Make us worthy of your gifts, O Lord, overlooking our transgressions; give healing through faith to them that accept your blessing, O Immortal One.

Then the Priest kisses the Precious Cross and blesses all the people, and he sprinkles all with the Holy Water, the Altar, and all the Temple. Meanwhile the Choir sings the following Troparia:

Tone 4

O holy Lord God, who is a fountain of healing, and gives healing to all that ask; You the same Lord has said to us: Lo! To you and your fellows has been given power over all unclean spirits, to drive them off with healing and free from every ill and wound; wherefore, abiding in that command, give healing of all our passions.

Glory to the Father and to the Son and to the Holy Spirit, both now and ever and to the ages of ages. Amen.

Priest:

Have mercy on us, O God, according to Your great Mercy, we beseech You: listen and have mercy.

People:

Lord have mercy. (And after each petition)

Priest:

Again we pray for our Bishop (Name) and for all our brethren in Christ.

Again we pray for mercy, life, peace, health, salvation, protection, pardon and remission of the sins of the servants of God, all pious and orthodox Christians who dwell in this city, and of the servants of God, the members, trustees, contributors, and benefactors of this Holy Church.

Furthermore, we pray that He will save this our city and this Holy Temple, and every city and countryside from pestilence, famine, earthquake, flood, fire, and the sword; from invasion of enemies, and from civil war; and that our good God, Who loves mankind, will be graciously favorable and easy to be entreated with, and will turn away all wrath stirred up against us and deliver us from all His righteous chastisement which impends against us, and have mercy on us.

Again we pray that the Lord our God listens to the voice of the supplication of us sinners, and has mercy on us.

Priest:

Hear us, O God our Savior, the Hope of all the ends of the earth and of those far off at sea, or in the air: show mercy, show mercy O Master, upon our sins, and have mercy on us. For You are a merciful God and love mankind, and to You do we send up all Glory: to the Father, and to the Son, and to the Holy Spirit, both now and ever, and to the ages of ages. Amen.

Apolysis

Glory to You, O Christ our God and our Hope, glory to You. Christ our true God, have mercy on us and save us, as our good and loving Lord.

Through the prayers of our holy Fathers, Lord Jesus Christ, our God, have mercy on us and save us.

People:

Amen.

Blessing of the St. Benedict Medal

In the Name of Jesus Christ our Lord. Amen.

V. Our help is in the name of the Lord.
R. Who made heaven and earth.

In the name of God the Father + almighty, who made heaven and earth, the seas and all that is in them, I exorcise these medals against the power and attacks of the evil one. May all who use these medals devoutly be blessed with health of soul and body. In the name of the Father +almighty, of the Son + Jesus Christ our Lord, and of the Holy + Spirit the Paraclete, and in the love of the same Lord Jesus Christ who will come on the last day to judge the living and the dead, and the world by fire.
Amen.

Let us pray. Almighty God, the boundless source of all good things, we humbly ask that, through the intercession of Saint Benedict, you pour out your blessings + upon these medals. May those who use them devoutly and earnestly strive to perform good works be blessed by you with health of soul and body, the grace of a holy life, and remission of the temporal punishment due to sin.

May they also with the help of your merciful love, resist the temptation of the evil one and strive to exercise true charity and justice toward all, so that one day they may appear sinless and holy in your sight. This we ask through Christ our Lord.
Amen.

The medals are then sprinkled with holy water.

Priest's Private Prayers at Holy Communion

Vesting Prayers

As each article of vestment is put on the following should be prayed:

Deacon:
Alb/Surplice: I will greatly rejoice in the Lord, My soul shall be joyful in my God; For He has clothed me with the garments of salvation, He has covered me with the robe of righteousness, As a bridegroom decks *himself* with ornaments, And as a bride adorns *herself* with her jewels. (Is. 61.10)

Stole: Jesus said, "Take my yoke upon you, and learn from me, for I am gentle and lowly in heart, and you will find rest for your souls. For my yoke is easy, and my burden is light." (Matt. 11.29-30)

Priest:
The Alb: I will greatly rejoice in the LORD; my soul shall exult in my God, for he has clothed me with the garments of salvation; he has covered me with the robe of righteousness, as a bridegroom decks himself like a priest with a beautiful headdress, and as a bride adorns herself with her jewels. (Isaiah 61.10)

The Stole: Blessed is our God who pours out his grace upon His priests. It is like the precious oil on the head, running down on the beard, on the beard of Aaron, running down to the fringe of his garments. (Ps 133.2; Exodus 29.7)

The Belt: Blessed is our God who girds me with strength and makes my way blameless. (Ps 18.32)

The Chasuble: Your priests, O Lord, shall be clothed with righteousness, and your holy ones shall rejoice with joy. (Ps 132.7, 16)

Entering the Altar

I will enter into your house by your lovingkindness. I will worship in reverent awe toward your holy temple. (Ps 5.7)

Or

In the multitude of Your mercies, O Lord, I go unto Your Altar. O save and deliver me for Your tender mercies' sake. Amen.

Or

Send out your light and your truth; let them lead me; let them bring me to your holy hill and to your dwelling! Then I will go to the altar of God, to God my exceeding joy. (Ps 43.3-5)

Incense

The incense to be offered shall be brought to the priest and he shall make the sign of the Cross over it and shall pray:

O Lord, grant to + bless this incense, and accept it as a sweet smelling savour, and kindle in our hearts the fire of Your love, through Jesus Christ our Lord. Amen.

At the Lavabo

I wash my hands in innocence and go around your altar, O Lord, proclaiming thanksgiving aloud, and telling all your wondrous deeds. O Lord, I love your Sanctuary and the place where your glory dwells. Do not sweep my soul away with sinners, nor my life with bloodthirsty men, in whose hands are evil devices, and whose right hands are full of bribes. But as for me, I shall walk in my integrity; redeem me, and be gracious to me. My foot stands on level ground; in the Church I will bless the Lord. (Ps 26.6-12)

Preparing the Bread and Wine

The priest places the Bread upon the Paten and prays:

He was oppressed, and he was afflicted, yet he opened not his mouth; like a lamb that is led to the slaughter, and like a sheep that before its shearers is silent, so he opened not his mouth.
By oppression and judgment he was taken away; and as for his generation, who considered that he was cut off out of the land of the living, stricken for the transgression of my people? (Isaiah 53.7-8)

The priest pours the Wine and Water into the Chalice and prays:

Priest: But one of the soldiers pierced his side with a spear, and at once there came out blood and water. He who saw it has borne witness—his testimony is true, and he knows that he is telling the truth—that you also may believe. (John 19.34-35)

The celebrant prays as he covers the chalice and paten:

Your steadfast love is great to the heavens, your faithfulness to the clouds. Be exalted, O God, above the heavens! Let your glory be over all the earth! (Psalm 57.10-11)

[If incense is used the priest should <u>cense</u> the Holy Gifts to be offered nine times.]

This service may be accomplished before the service begins, during the Holy Communion, or during the Litany if there be a Deacon to pray the Litany.

At the Beginning of Any Service

The Priest prays out loud:
In the Name + of the Father and of the Son and of the Holy Spirit, Ever One God. Amen.

First Approach to the Altar

Taking his position at the center of the Altar, the priest prays <u>quietly</u> to himself:

Take away from us, O Lord, we beg of You, our iniquities, that we may enter with pure hearts into Your most Holy Place. Amen.

Stretch forth Your hand. O Lord, from Your holy dwelling place on high and strengthen me for this, Your appointed service, that standing without condemnation in Your dread sanctuary I may offer the bloodless sacrifice of thanksgiving; for Yours in the power and the glory, forever. Amen.

PRAYERS, EPISTLES, AND GOSPELS FOR VARIOUS OCCASIONS

A Saint's Day

The Prayer.

ALMIGHTY and everlasting God, who kindles the flame of Your love in the hearts of the Saints: grant to us, Your humble servants, the same faith and power of love; that as we rejoice in their triumphs, we may profit by their examples; through Jesus Christ our Lord. *Amen.*

Or this.

O ALMIGHTY God, Who has called us to faith in You, and has surrounded us with so great a cloud of witnesses: grant that we, encouraged by the good examples of Your Saints, and especially of Your servant [*N.*], may persevere in running the race that is set before us, until at length, through Your mercy, we, with them, attain to Your eternal joy; through Him who is the author and finisher of our faith, Your Son Jesus Christ our Lord. *Amen.*

The Epistle. Hebrews 12.1-2

Therefore, since we also have such a great cloud of witnesses surrounding us, let's rid ourselves of every obstacle and the sin which so easily entangles us, and let's run with endurance the race that is set before us, looking only at Jesus, the originator and perfecter of the faith, who for the joy set before Him endured the cross, despising the shame, and has sat down at the right hand of the throne of God.

The Gospel. St Matthew 25.31-40

"But when the Son of Man comes in His glory, and all the angels with Him, then He will sit on His glorious throne. And all the nations will be gathered before Him; and He will separate them from one another, just as the shepherd separates the sheep from the goats; and

He will put the sheep on His right, but the goats on the left. Then the King will say to those on His right, 'Come, you who are blessed of My Father, inherit the kingdom prepared for you from the foundation of the world. For I was hungry, and you gave Me *something* to eat; I was thirsty, and you gave Me *something* to drink; I was a stranger, and you invited Me in; naked, and you clothed Me; I was sick, and you visited Me; I was in prison, and you came to Me.' Then the righteous will answer Him, 'Lord, when did we see You hungry, and feed You, or thirsty, and give You *something* to drink? And when did we see You *as* a stranger, and invite You in, or naked, and clothe You? And when did we see You sick, or in prison, and come to You?' And the King will answer and say to them, 'Truly I say to you, to the extent that you did *it* for one of the least of these brothers *or sisters* of Mine, you did *it* for Me.'"

Feast of the Dedication of a Church

The Prayer.

O GOD, Whom year by year we praise for the dedication of this church: we ask You to hear the prayers of Your people, and grant that whosoever shall worship before You in this place, may obtain Your merciful aid and protection; through Jesus Christ our Lord. *Amen.*

The Epistle. 1 St Peter 2.1-5

Therefore, rid *yourselves* of all malice and all deceit and hypocrisy and envy and all slander, and like newborn babies, long for the pure milk of the word, so that by it you may grow in respect to salvation, if you have tasted the kindness of the Lord. And coming to Him as to a living stone which has been rejected by people, but is choice and precious in the sight of God, you also, as living stones, are being built up as a spiritual house for a holy priesthood, to offer spiritual sacrifices that are acceptable to God through Jesus Christ.

The Gospel. St Matthew 21.12-16

And Jesus entered the temple *area* and drove out all those who were selling and buying on the temple *grounds*, and He overturned the tables of the money changers and the seats of those who were selling doves. And He *said to them, "It is written: 'MY HOUSE WILL BE CALLED A HOUSE OF PRAYER'; but you are making it a DEN OF ROBBERS." And *those who were* blind and *those who* limped came to Him in the temple *area*, and He healed them. But when the chief priests and the scribes saw the wonderful things that He had done, and the children who were shouting in the temple *area*, "Hosanna to the Son of David," they became indignant, and they said to Him, "Do You hear what these *children* are saying?" And Jesus *said to them, "Yes. Have you never read, 'FROM THE MOUTHS OF INFANTS AND NURSING BABIES YOU HAVE PREPARED PRAISE FOR YOURSELF'?"

The Recurring Fasts also called Ember Days

At the Four Seasons
(*These days of fasting and prayer occur on the Wednesday, Friday, and Saturday following the third Sunday of Advent, the first Sunday of Lent, Pentecost Sunday, and the third Sunday of September.*)

O ALMIGHTY God, Who has committed to the hands of men the ministry of reconciliation: we humbly entreat You, by the inspiration of Your Holy Spirit, to put it into the hearts of many to offer themselves for this ministry; that thereby mankind may be drawn to Your blessed kingdom; through Jesus Christ our Lord. *Amen.*
The Epistle. Acts 13.44-49

The next Sabbath almost the whole city gathered to hear the word of the Lord. But when the Jews saw the crowds, they were filled with jealousy and began to contradict what was spoken by Paul, reviling him. And Paul and Barnabas spoke out boldly, saying, "It was necessary that the word of God be spoken first to you. Since you thrust it aside and judge yourselves unworthy of eternal life, behold, we are turning to the Gentiles. For so the Lord has commanded us, saying, "'I have made you a light for the Gentiles, that you may bring salvation to the ends of the earth.'" And when the Gentiles heard this, they began rejoicing and glorifying the word of the Lord, and as many as were appointed to eternal life believed. And the word of the Lord was spreading throughout the whole region.

The Gospel. St Luke 4.16-21

And Jesus came to Nazareth, where He had been brought up; and as was His custom, He entered the synagogue on the Sabbath, and stood up to read. And the scroll of Isaiah the prophet was handed to Him. And He unrolled the scroll and found the place where it was written: "THE SPIRIT OF THE LORD IS UPON ME, BECAUSE HE ANOINTED ME TO BRING GOOD NEWS TO THE POOR. HE HAS SENT ME TO PROCLAIM RELEASE TO CAPTIVES, AND RECOVERY OF SIGHT TO THE BLIND, TO SET FREE THOSE WHO ARE OPPRESSED, TO PROCLAIM THE FAVORABLE YEAR OF THE LORD." And He rolled up the scroll, gave it back to the attendant, and sat down; and the eyes of all *the people* in the synagogue were intently directed at Him. Now He began to say to them, "Today this Scripture has been fulfilled in your hearing."

The Asking Days also called Rogation Days

Being the Three Days before Ascension Day
(Rogation comes from a Latin word that means "to ask" and
are days of fasting and asking the Lord for blessings)

The Prayer.

ALMIGHTY God, Lord of heaven and earth; we ask You to pour forth Your blessing upon this land, and to give us a fruitful season: that we, constantly receiving Your bounty, may evermore give thanks unto You in Your holy Church; through Jesus Christ our Lord. *Amen.*

The Epistle. Ezekiel 34.25-31

"I will make a covenant of peace with them and eliminate harmful animals from the land, so that they may live securely in the wilderness and sleep in the woods. I will make them and the places around My hill a blessing. And I will make showers fall in their season; they will be showers of blessing. Also the tree of the field will yield its fruit and the earth will yield its produce, and they will be secure on their land. Then they will know that I am the LORD, when I have broken the bars of their yoke and have saved them from the hand of those who enslaved them. They will no longer be plunder to the nations, and the animals of the earth will not devour them; but they will live securely, and no one will make *them* afraid. I will establish for them a renowned planting place, and they will not again be victims of famine in the land, and they will not endure the insults of the nations anymore. Then they will know that I, the LORD their God, am with them, and that they, the house of Israel, are My people," declares the Lord GOD. "As for you, My sheep, the sheep of My pasture, you are mankind, *and* I am your God," declares the Lord GOD.

The Gospel. St Luke 11.5-13

"And Jesus said to them, "Suppose one of you has a friend, and goes to him at midnight and says to him, 'Friend, lend me three loaves, because a friend of mine has come to me from a journey and I have nothing to serve him'; and from inside he answers and says, 'Do not bother me; the door has already been shut and my children and I are in bed; I cannot get up and give you *anything*.' I tell you, even if he will not get up and give him *anything just* because he is his friend, yet because of his shamelessness he will get up and give him as much as he needs. So I say to you, ask, and it will be given to you; seek, and you will find; knock, and it will be opened to you. For everyone who asks receives, and the one who seeks finds, and to the one who knocks, it will be opened. Now which one of you fathers will his son ask for a fish, and instead of a fish, he will give him a snake? Or he will even ask for an egg, *and his father* will give him a scorpion? So if you, *despite* being evil, know how to give good gifts to your children, how much more will your heavenly Father give the Holy Spirit to those who ask Him?"

Independence Day

The Prayer.

O ETERNAL God, through Whose mighty power our fathers won their liberties of old; Grant, we entreat You, that we and all the people of this land may have grace to maintain these liberties in righteousness and peace; through Jesus Christ our Lord. *Amen.*

The Epistle. Deuteronomy 10.17-21

For the LORD your God is the God of gods and the Lord of lords, the great, the mighty, and the awesome God, who does not show partiality, nor take a bribe. He executes justice for the orphan and the widow, and shows His love for the stranger by giving him food and clothing. So show your love for the stranger, for you were strangers in the land of Egypt. You shall fear the LORD your God; you shall serve Him, and cling to Him, and you shall swear by His name. He is your glory and He is your God, who has done these great and awesome things for you which your eyes have seen.

The Gospel. St Matthew 5.43-48

"You have heard that it was said, 'YOU SHALL LOVE YOUR NEIGHBOR and hate your enemy.' But I say to you, love your enemies and pray for those who persecute you, so that you may prove yourselves to be sons of your Father who is in heaven; for He causes His sun to rise on *the* evil and *the* good, and sends rain on *the* righteous and *the* unrighteous. For if you love those who love you, what reward do you have? Even the tax collectors, do they not do the same? And if you greet only your brothers *and sisters*, what more are you doing *than others*? Even the Gentiles, do they not do the same? Therefore you shall be perfect, as your heavenly Father is perfect.

Thanksgiving Day

The Thanksgiving. Psalm 147.1-3, 7-9, 12-14
This shall be said instead of Psalm 95 O Come Let Us Sing (Venite)

147 Praise the LORD!
For it is good to sing praises to our God;
For it is pleasant *and* praise is beautiful.
2 The LORD builds up Jerusalem;
He gathers the outcasts of Israel.
3 He heals the brokenhearted
And binds up their wounds.
Sing to the LORD with thanksgiving;
Sing praises to our God on the lyre;

8 *It is* He who covers the heavens with clouds,
Who provides rain for the earth,
Who makes grass sprout on the mountains.
9 *It is* He who gives an animal its food,
And feeds young ravens that cry.
12 Praise the LORD, Jerusalem!
Praise your God, Zion!
13 For He has strengthened the bars of your gates;
He has blessed your sons among you.
14 He makes peace in your borders;
He satisfies you with the finest of the wheat.

The Prayer.

O MOST merciful Father, Who has blessed the labors of farmers in the returns of the fruits of the earth: we give You humble and hearty thanks for this Your bounty; entreating You to continue Your loving-kindness to us, that our land may still yield her increase, to Your glory and our comfort; through Jesus Christ our Lord. *Amen.*

The Epistle. St James 1.16-27

Do not be deceived, my beloved brothers *and sisters*. Every good thing given and every perfect gift is from above, coming down from the Father of lights, with whom there is no variation or shifting shadow. In the exercise of His will He gave us birth by the word of truth, so that we would be a kind of first fruits among His creatures. You know *this*, my beloved brothers *and sisters*. Now everyone must be quick to hear, slow to speak, *and* slow to anger; for a man's anger does not bring about the righteousness of God. Therefore, ridding *yourselves* of all filthiness and *all* that remains of wickedness, in humility receive the word implanted, which is able to save your souls. But prove yourselves doers of the word, and not just hearers who deceive themselves. For if anyone is a hearer of the word and not a doer, he is like a man who looks at his natural face in a mirror; for *once* he has looked at himself and gone away, he has immediately forgotten what kind of person he was. But one who has looked intently at the perfect law, the *law* of freedom, and has continued *in it*, not having become a forgetful hearer but an active doer, this person will be blessed in what he does. If anyone thinks himself to be religious, yet does not bridle his tongue but deceives his *own* heart, this person's religion is worthless. Pure and undefiled religion in the sight of *our* God and Father is this: to visit orphans and widows in their distress, *and* to keep oneself unstained by the world.

The Gospel. St Matthew 6.25-34

"For this reason I say to you, do not be worried about your life, *as to* what you will eat or what you will drink; nor for your body, *as to* what you will put on. Is life not more than food, and the body more than clothing? Look at the birds of the sky, that they do not sow, nor reap, nor gather *crops* into barns, and *yet* your heavenly Father feeds them. Are you not much more important than they? And which of you by worrying can add a single day to his life's span? And why are you worried about clothing? Notice how the lilies of the field grow; they do not labor nor do they spin *thread for cloth*, yet I say to you that not even Solomon in all his glory clothed himself like one of these. But if God so clothes the grass of the field, which is *alive* today and tomorrow is thrown into the furnace, *will He* not much more *clothe* you? You of little faith! Do not worry then, saying, 'What are we to eat?' or 'What are we to drink?' or 'What are we to wear for clothing?' For the Gentiles eagerly seek all these things; for your heavenly Father knows that you need all these things. But seek first His kingdom and His righteousness, and all these things will be provided to you. So do not worry about tomorrow; for tomorrow will worry about itself. Each day has enough trouble of its own."

At a Marriage

The Prayer.

O ETERNAL God, we humbly entreat You to look favorably upon these Your servants now (*or* about to be) joined in wedlock according to Your holy ordinance: and grant that they, seeking first Your kingdom and Your righteousness, may obtain the manifold blessings of Your grace; through Jesus Christ our Lord. *Amen.*

The Epistle. Ephesians 5.20-33

Always give thanks for all things in the name of our Lord Jesus Christ to *our* God and Father; and subject yourselves to one another in the fear of Christ. Wives, *subject yourselves* to your own husbands, as to the Lord. For the husband is the head of the wife, as Christ also is the head of the church, He Himself *being* the Savior of the body. But as the church is subject to Christ, so also the wives *ought to be* to their husbands in everything. Husbands, love your wives, just as Christ also loved the church and gave Himself up for her, so that He might sanctify her, having cleansed her by the washing of water with the word, that He might present to Himself the church in all her glory, having no spot or wrinkle or any such thing; but that she would be holy and blameless. So husbands also ought to love their own wives as their own bodies. He who loves his own wife loves himself; for no one ever hated his own flesh, but nourishes and cherishes it, just as Christ also *does* the church, because we are parts of His body. FOR THIS REASON A MAN SHALL LEAVE HIS FATHER AND HIS MOTHER AND BE JOINED TO HIS WIFE, AND THE TWO SHALL BECOME ONE FLESH. This mystery is great; but I am speaking with reference to Christ and the church. Nevertheless, as for you individually, each *husband* is to love his own wife the same as himself, and the wife *must see to it* that she respects her husband.

The Gospel. St Matthew 19.4-6

And Jesus answered and said, "Have you not read that He who created *them* from the beginning MADE THEM MALE AND FEMALE, and said, 'FOR THIS REASON A MAN SHALL LEAVE HIS FATHER AND HIS MOTHER AND BE JOINED TO HIS WIFE, AND THE TWO SHALL BECOME ONE FLESH'? So they are no longer two, but one flesh. Therefore, what God has joined together, no person is to separate."

At the Burial of the Dead

The Prayer.

O ETERNAL Lord God, who holds all souls in life: we implore You to grant to Your whole Church in paradise and on earth, Your light and Your peace; and grant that we, following the good examples of those who have served You here and are now at rest, may at the last enter with them into Your unending joy; through Jesus Christ our Lord. *Amen.*

Or this prayer

O GOD, Whose mercies cannot be numbered: accept our prayers on behalf of the soul of Your servant who has departed, and grant *him* an entrance into the land of light and joy, in the fellowship of Your saints; through Jesus Christ our Lord. *Amen.*

The Epistle. 1 Thessalonians 4.13-18

But we do not want you to be uninformed, brothers *and sisters*, about those who are asleep, so that you will not grieve as indeed the rest *of mankind do*, who have no hope. For if we believe that Jesus died and rose *from the dead*, so also God will bring with Him those who have fallen asleep through Jesus. For we say this to you by the word of the Lord, that we who are alive and remain until the coming of the Lord will not precede those who have fallen asleep. For the Lord Himself will descend from heaven with a shout, with the voice of *the* archangel and with the trumpet of God, and the dead in Christ will rise first. Then we who are alive, who remain, will be caught up together with them in the clouds to meet the Lord in the air, and so we will always be with the Lord. Therefore, comfort one another with these words.

The Gospel. St John 6.37-40

Jesus said, "Everyone that the Father gives Me will come to Me, and the one who comes to Me I certainly will not cast out. For I have come down from heaven, not to do My own will, but the will of Him who sent Me. And this is the will of Him who sent Me, that of everything that He has given Me I will lose nothing, but will raise it up on the last day. For this is the will of My Father, that everyone who sees the Son and believes in Him will have eternal life, and I Myself will raise him up on the last day."

ADDITIONAL PRAYERS (Collects)

To be used after the Collects of Morning or Evening Prayer, or Communion, at the discretion of the Minister.

O LORD Jesus Christ, who said unto Your Apostles, Peace I leave with you, My peace I give unto you: regard not our sins, but the faith of Your Church instead; and grant to it that peace and unity which is according to Your will, who lives and reigns with the Father and the Holy Spirit, one God, world without end. *Amen.*

ASSIST us mercifully, O Lord, in these our supplications and prayers, and dispose the way of Your servants towards the attainment of everlasting salvation; that, among all the changes and chances of this mortal life, they may ever be defended by Your most gracious and ready help; through Jesus Christ our Lord. *Amen.*

WE ASK You, Almighty God, to grant that the words which we have heard this day with our outward ears, may, through Your grace, be so grafted inwardly in our hearts, that they may bring forth in us the fruit of good living, to the honor and praise of Your Name; through Jesus Christ our Lord. *Amen.*

DIRECT us, O Lord, in all our doings, with Your most gracious favor, and help us to advance with Your continual help, that in all our works begun, continued, and ended in You, we may glorify Your holy Name, and finally, by Your mercy, obtain everlasting life; through Jesus Christ our Lord. *Amen.*

ALMIGHTY God, the fountain of all wisdom, who knows our needs before we ask, and our ignorance in asking: we implore You to have compassion upon our infirmities; and those things which for our unworthiness we dare not ask, and for our blindness we cannot ask, grant to give us, for the worthiness of Your Son Jesus Christ our Lord. *Amen.*

ALMIGHTY God, who has promised to hear the petitions of those who ask in Your Son's Name: we entreat You to mercifully incline Your ears to us who have now made our prayers and supplications unto You; and grant that those things which we have faithfully asked according to Your will, may effectually be obtained, to the relief of our needs, and to the setting forth of Your glory; through Jesus Christ our Lord. *Amen.*

SUPPLEMENTARY PRAYERS AND THANKSGIVINGS

For the Government

MOST gracious God, we humbly entreat You, as for the people of this nation in general, so especially for their rulers and representatives in the government whose hearts are a stream of water in the hand of You O LORD, and You turn them wherever You will, that You would be pleased to direct all their consultations and prosper them according to Your Sovereign will, to the advancement of Your glory, the good of Your Church, the safety, honor, and welfare of Your people; that all things may be so ordered and settled by their endeavors, upon the best and surest foundations, that peace and happiness, truth and justice, religion and piety, may be established among us for all generations. These and all other indispensible things, for them, and for us, and Your whole Church, we humbly beg in the Name and mediation of Jesus Christ, our most blessed Lord and Savior. *Amen.*

For the State or Regional Government

O GOD, the fountain of wisdom, Whose statutes are good and gracious and Whose law is truth: We implore You so to guide and bless the government of this State (Region, etc.) that it may ordain for our governance only such things as are pleasing to You, to the glory of Your Name and the welfare of the people; through Jesus Christ, Your Son, our Lord. *Amen.*

For Courts of Justice

ALMIGHTY God, who sits in the throne judging right: we humbly plead with You to bless the courts of justice and the magistrates in all this land; and give unto them the spirit of wisdom and understanding, that they may discern the truth and impartially administer the law in the fear of You alone; through him who shall come to be our judge, Your Son, our Savior, Jesus Christ. *Amen.*

For Our Country

ALMIGHTY God, who has given us this good land for our heritage: we humbly request of You that we may always prove ourselves a people mindful of Your favor and glad to do Your will. Bless our land with honorable industry, sound learning, and pure manners. Save us from violence, discord, and confusion; from pride and arrogance, and from every evil way. Defend our liberties, and fashion into one united people the multitudes brought here out of many kindreds and tongues. Endue with the spirit of wisdom those to whom in Your Name we entrust the authority of government, that there may be justice and peace at home, and that, through obedience to Your law, we may show forth Your praise among the nations of the earth. In the time of prosperity, fill our hearts with thankfulness, and in the day of trouble, do not allow our trust in You to fail; all which we ask through Jesus Christ our Lord. *Amen.*

A Prayer to be used at the Meetings of Convention

ALMIGHTY and everlasting God, who by Your Holy Spirit presided in the Council of the blessed Apostles, and has promised, through Your Son Jesus Christ, to be with Your Church to the end of the world: we implore You to be with the Council of Your Church assembled here in your Name and Presence. Save us from all error, ignorance, pride, and prejudice; and of Your great mercy vouchsafe, we pray to You, to so direct, sanctify, and govern us in our work, by the mighty power of the Holy Spirit, that the comfortable Gospel of Christ may be truly preached, truly received, and truly followed, in all places, to the breaking down the kingdom of sin, Satan, and death; till at length the whole of Your dispersed sheep, being gathered into one fold, shall become partakers of everlasting life; through the merits and death of Jesus Christ our Savior. *Amen.*

During, or before, the session of any General or Diocesan Convention, the above Prayer may be used by all Congregations of this Church. or of the Diocese concerned; the clause, here assembled in Your Name, being changed to now assembled [or about to assemble] in Your Name and Presence; and the clause, govern us in our work, to govern them in their work.

For the Church

O GRACIOUS Father, we humbly entreat You for Your holy Church Catholic*: that You would be pleased to fill it with all truth, in all peace. Where it is corrupt, purify it; where it is in error, direct it; where in anything it is amiss, reform it. Where it is right, establish it; where it is in want, provide for it; where it is divided, reunite it; for the sake of Him who died and rose again, and ever lives to make intercession for us, Jesus Christ, Your Son, our Lord. *Amen.*
The word catholic comes from the Greek word katholicos found in the Bible and means universal, everywhere, the entirety of the truth, the entire body of believing Christians, the whole, all-inclusive, relating to all, broad, wide-spread, etc. The Church of Jesus Christ is Catholic.

For the Unity of God's People

O GOD, the Father of our Lord Jesus Christ, our only Savior, the Prince of Peace: give us grace to seriously lay to heart the great dangers we are in by our unhappy divisions. Take away all hatred and prejudice, and whatsoever else may hinder us from godly, union and concord: that as there is but one Body and one Spirit, and one hope of our calling, one Lord, one Faith, one Baptism, one God and Father of us all, so we may be all of one heart and of one soul, united in one holy bond of truth and peace, of faith and charity, and may with one mind and one mouth glorify You; through Jesus Christ our Lord. *Amen.*

For Missions

O GOD, who has made of one blood all nations of men for to dwell on the face of the whole earth, and sent Your blessed Son to preach peace to them that are far off and to them that are near: grant that all men everywhere may seek after You and find You. Bring the nations into Your fold, pour out Your Spirit upon all flesh, and hasten Your kingdom; through the same Your Son Jesus Christ our Lord. *Amen.*

Or this

ALMIGHTY God, whose compassions fail not, and whose loving-kindness reaches unto the world's end: we give You humble thanks for opening heathen lands to the light of Your truth; for making paths in the deep waters and highways in the desert; and for planting Your Church in all the earth. Grant, we beseech You, unto us Your servants, that with lively faith we may labor abundantly to make known to all men Your blessed gift of eternal life; through Jesus Christ our Lord. *Amen.*

For those who are to be admitted into Holy Orders.

To be used in the Weeks preceding the stated Times of Ordination.

ALMIGHTY God, our heavenly Father, who has purchased to Yourself an universal Church by the precious blood of Your dear Son: Mercifully look upon the same, and at this time so guide and govern the minds of Your servants the Bishops and Pastors of Your flock, that they may lay hands suddenly on no man, but faithfully and wisely make choice of fit persons, to serve in the sacred Ministry of Your Church, And to those who shall be ordained to any holy function, give Your grace and heavenly benediction; that both by their life and doctrine they may show forth Your glory, and set forward the salvation of all men; through Jesus Christ our Lord. *Amen.*

Or this

ALMIGHTY God, the giver of all good gifts, who of Your divine providence has appointed various Orders in Your Church: Give Your grace, we humbly ask You, to all those who are to be called to any office and administration in the same; and so replenish them with the truth of Your doctrine, and endue them with innocency of life, that they may faithfully serve before You, to the glory of Your great Name, and the benefit of Your holy Church; through Jesus Christ our Lord. *Amen.*

For the Increase of the Ministry

O ALMIGHTY God, look mercifully upon the world which You have redeemed by the blood of Your dear Son, and incline the hearts of many to dedicate themselves to the sacred ministry of Your Church; through the same Your Son Jesus Christ our Lord. *Amen.*

For Fruitful Seasons

To be used on Rogation-Sunday and the Rogation-days

ALMIGHTY God, who has blessed the earth that it should be fruitful and bring forth whatsoever is needful for the life of man, and has commanded us to work with quietness, and eat our own bread: Bless the labors of the farmer, and grant such seasonable weather that we may gather in the fruits of the earth, and ever rejoice in Your goodness, to the praise of Your holy Name; through Jesus Christ our Lord. *Amen.*

Or this

O GRACIOUS Father, who opens Your hand and fills all things living with plenteousness: We implore You of Your infinite goodness to hear us, who now make our prayers and supplications unto You. Remember not our sins, but Your promises of mercy. Condescend to bless the lands and multiply the harvests of the world. Let Your breath go forth that it may renew the face of the earth. Show Your loving-kindness, that our land may give her increase; and so fill us with good things that the poor and needy may give thanks unto Your Name; through Christ our Lord. *Amen.*

For Rain

O GOD, heavenly Father, who by Your Son Jesus Christ has promised to all those who seek Your kingdom and its righteousness, all things necessary to their bodily sustenance: We pray for You to send us, in this our time of need, such moderate rain and showers, that we may receive the fruits of the earth to our comfort, and to Your honor; through Jesus Christ our Lord. *Amen.*

For Fair Weather

ALMIGHTY and most merciful Father, we humbly pray that You, out of Your great goodness, restrain those immoderate rains, wherewith You have afflicted us. And we pray You to send us such appropriate weather, that the earth in due time may yield her increase for our use and benefit; through Jesus Christ our Lord. *Amen.*

In Time of Dearth and Famine

O GOD, heavenly Father, whose gift it is that the rain does fall, and the earth bring forth her increase: We implore You to behold the afflictions of Your people; increase the fruits of the earth by Your heavenly blessing; and grant that the scarcity and dearth, which we now most justly suffer for our sins, may, through Your goodness, be mercifully turned into plenty; for the love of Jesus Christ our Lord, to whom, with You and the Holy Spirit, be all honor and glory, now and forever. *Amen.*

In Time of War and Tumults

ALMIGHTY God, the supreme Governor of all things, whose power no creature is able to resist, to whom it belongs justly to punish sinners, and to be merciful to those who truly repent: save and deliver us, we humbly entreat You, from the hands of our enemies; that we, being armed with Your defense, may be preserved evermore from all perils to glorify You, who are the only giver of all victory; through the merits of Your Son, Jesus Christ our Lord. *Amen.*

In Time of Calamity

O GOD, merciful and compassionate, who are ever ready to hear the prayers of those who put their trust in You: graciously listen to us who call upon You, and grant us Your help in this our need; through Jesus Christ our Lord. *Amen.*

For the Army and Marines

O LORD God of Hosts, stretch forth, we pray to You, Your almighty arm to strengthen and protect the soldiers and marines of our country: support them in the day of battle, and in the time of peace keep them safe from all evil; endue them with courage and loyalty; and grant that in all things they may serve without reproach; through Jesus Christ our Lord. *Amen.*

For the Navy

O ETERNAL Lord God, who alone spreads out the heavens, and rules the raging of the sea: we ask You to grant to take into Your almighty and most gracious protection our country's Navy, and all who serve therein. Preserve them from the dangers of the sea, and from the violence of the enemy; that they may be a safeguard unto our Nation, and a security for such as pass on the seas upon their lawful occasions; that the inhabitants of our land may in peace and quietness serve You our God, to the glory of Your Name; through Jesus Christ our Lord. *Amen.*

For the Air Force

O Lord our Governor, who has given humankind dominion over earth, air and sea; we ask you to look favorably upon your servants who are called to serve their country in the Air Force. Give your servants courage, a steady nerve and a ready mind. Sustain them in days of preparation, in the daily round of routine servicing and weary waiting. Be with them we pray in all times of sudden peril, and grant that under your mighty protection they may be preserved in body, mind and spirit. We ask this prayer through Jesus Christ our Lord. *Amen.*

For the Coast Guard

Almighty and Everlasting God, Whose hand stills the tumult of the deep, we offer our prayers for those who serve in our Coast Guard. We are mindful of their traditions of selfless service to the seafarers who make their ways to appointed ports. Employ their devotions of good ends as they track the weather and search for the seas for those in extremity of storm, shipwreck or battle. Make their soundings and markings sure that safe passages may be found by those who go down to the sea in ships. Uphold them, O Lord, as they stand guard over our coasts and the bulwarks of our freedoms. Graciously deliver them from threatening calamities in all their perilous voyages. Bless the keepers of the lights and You be their close friend in lonely watches. Keep the beacons of honor and duty burning that they may reach the home port with duty well performed, in service to Thee and our land. *Amen.*

For Astronauts

ALMIGHTY God Who is everywhere present and fills all things, we implore You for our astronauts that the Presence of God surrounds them; the Love of God enfolds them; the Power of God protects them; the Angels of God watch over them; the Will of God guides them; the Life of Christ our God flows through them; the Laws of God direct them; the Power of God abides within them; the Joy of God uplifts them; the Strength of God renews them; the Glory of God inspires them; and that they be assured that wherever they are, God is; through our Lord Jesus Christ. *Amen.*

Memorial Days

ALMIGHTY God, our heavenly Father, in whose hands are the living and the dead: we give You thanks for all of Your servants who have laid down their lives in the service of our country. Grant to them Your mercy and the light of Your presence, that the good work which You has begun in them may be perfected; through Jesus Christ Your Son our Lord. *Amen.*

For Schools, Colleges, and Universities

ALMIGHTY God, we beseech You, with Your gracious favor, to behold our universities, colleges, and schools, that knowledge may be increased among us, and all good learning flourish and abound; bless all who teach and all who learn; and grant that in humility of heart they may ever look unto You, who art the fountain of all wisdom; through Jesus Christ our Lord. *Amen.*

For Religious Education

ALMIGHTY God, our Heavenly Father, who has committed to Your Holy Church the care and nurture of Your people, young to elderly: enlighten with Your wisdom those who teach and those who learn; that, rejoicing in the knowledge of Your truth, they may worship You and serve You from generation to generation; through Jesus Christ our Lord. *Amen.*

For Children

O LORD, Jesus Christ, who embraces children with the arms of Your mercy, and makes them living members of Your Church: give them grace, we pray You, to stand fast in Your faith, to obey Your word, and to abide in Your love; that being made strong by Your Holy Spirit they may resist temptation and overcome evil; and may rejoice in the life that now is, and dwell with You in the life that is to come; through Your merits, O merciful Savior, who with the Father and the Holy Spirit lives and reigns one God, world without end. *Amen.*

For Those About to be Confirmed

O GOD, who through the teaching of Your Son Jesus Christ did prepare the disciples for the coming of the Comforter: make ready, we pray You, the hearts and minds of Your servants who at this time are seeking to be strengthened by the gift of the Holy Spirit through the laying on of hands, that, drawing near with penitent and faithful hearts, they may evermore be filled with the power of his divine indwelling; through the same Jesus Christ our Lord. *Amen.*

For Christian Service

O LORD our heavenly Father, whose blessed Son came not to be ministered unto, but to minister: we ask You to bless all who, following in his steps, give themselves to the service of their fellow men. Endue them with wisdom, patience, and courage, that they may strengthen the weak and raise up those who fall; and, being inspired by Your love, may minister in a worthy manner in Your Name to the suffering, the friendless, and the needy; for the sake of him who laid down his life for us, the same Your Son, our Savior, Jesus Christ. *Amen.*

For Social Justice

ALMIGHTY God, who has created man in Your own image: grant us grace fearlessly to contend against evil, and to make no peace with oppression; and, that we may reverently use our freedom, help us to employ it in the maintenance of justice among men and nations, to the glory of Your holy Name; through Jesus Christ our Lord. *Amen.*

For Every Man in his Work

ALMIGHTY God, our heavenly Father, who declares Your glory and shows forth Your handiwork in the heavens and in the earth; Deliver us, we beseech You, in our several callings, from the service of mammon, that we may do the work which You give us to do, in truth, in beauty, and in righteousness, with singleness of heart as Your servants, and to the benefit of our fellow men; for the sake of him who came among us as one that serves, Your Son, Jesus Christ our Lord. *Amen.*

For the Family of Nations

ALMIGHTY God, our heavenly Father, guide, we implore You, the Nations of the world into the way of justice and truth, and establish among them that peace which is the fruit of righteousness, that they may become the Kingdom of our Lord and Savior Jesus Christ. *Amen.*

In Time of Great Sickness and Mortality

O MOST mighty and merciful God, in this time of grievous sickness, we flee unto You for succor. Deliver us, we beg You, from our peril; give strength and skill to all those who minister to the sick; prosper the means made use of for their cure; and grant that, perceiving how frail and uncertain our life is, we may apply our hearts unto that heavenly wisdom which leads to eternal life; through Jesus Christ our Lord. *Amen.*

For a Sick Person

O FATHER of mercies and God of all comfort, our only help in time of need: we humbly ask You to behold, visit, and relieve Your sick servant

[N.] for whom our prayers are desired. Look upon *him* with the eyes of Your mercy; comfort *him* with a sense of Your goodness; preserve *him* from the temptations of the enemy; and give *him* patience under *his* affliction. In Your good time, restore *him* to health, and enable *him* to lead the remainder of *his* life in Your fear, and to Your glory; and grant that finally *he* may dwell with You in life everlasting; through Jesus Christ our Lord. *Amen.*

For a Sick Child

O HEAVENLY Father, watch with us, we pray You, over the sick child for whom our prayers are offered, and grant that *he* may be restored to that perfect health which it is Yours alone to give; through Jesus Christ our Lord. *Amen.*

For a Family at the Loss of a Loved One

O Lord, who loves mankind, in Your mercy, be with those of us who mourn the loss of our loved one. Under the shadow of Your wing let us hope, for You are the hope of all mankind. You will support us, when in our grief, our strength is small. When our strength is of You, it is true strength, but when our own, it is feebleness. We lean upon You who are our refreshment and true strength, for in You alone can our wearied, mourning spirits find rest. We are happy if You give comfort and peace. Preserve peace in our hearts, that peace which passes all understanding. Strengthen us who are in sorrow by the inward comfort of Your Holy Spirit. Help us to the place of perfect rest where we shall behold Your loving face and be satisfied by Your eternal fullness and comfort; we pray You through Your Holy Son Jesus. Amen.

For a Person under Affliction

O MERCIFUL God, and heavenly Father, who has taught us in Your holy Word that You do not willingly afflict or grieve the children of men: we plead with You to look with pity upon the sorrows of Your servant for whom our prayers are offered. Remember *him*, O Lord, in mercy; endue *his* soul with patience; comfort *him* with a sense of Your goodness; lift up Your countenance upon *him*, and give *him* peace; through Jesus Christ our Lord. *Amen.*

For a Person, or Persons, going to Sea

O ETERNAL God, who alone spreads out the heavens, and rules the raging of the sea: We commend to Your almighty protection, Your servant, for whose preservation on the great deep our prayers are desired. Guard him, we beseech You, from the dangers of the sea, from sickness, from the violence of enemies, and from every evil to which he may be exposed. Conduct him in safety to the haven where he would be, with a grateful sense of Your mercies; through Jesus Christ our Lord. *Amen.*

For Anyone Going Into Space

O ETERNAL God, who alone made the stars and spreads out the heavens: We commend to Your almighty protection, Your servant(s), for whose preservation in the great vastness of space our prayers are desired. Guard him (them), we beseech You, from the dangers of outer space, from sickness, from the violence of enemies, and from every evil to which he (they) may be exposed. Conduct him (them) in safety to the haven where he would be, with a grateful sense of Your mercies; through Jesus Christ our Lord. *Amen.*

For Prisoners

O GOD, who spares us when we deserve punishment, and in Your wrath remembers mercy: we humbly implore You, of Your goodness, to comfort and succor all prisoners [especially those who are condemned to die]. Give them a right understanding of themselves, and of Your promises; that, trusting wholly in Your mercy, they may not place their confidence anywhere but in You. Relieve the distressed, protect the innocent, awaken the guilty; and forasmuch as You alone bring light out of darkness, and good out of evil, grant to these Your servants, that by the power of Your Holy Spirit they may be set free from the chains of sin, and may be brought to newness of life; through Jesus Christ our Lord. *Amen.*

A Bidding Prayer

To be used before Sermons, or on Special Occasions.

GOOD Christian People, I bid your prayers for Christ's holy Catholic Church, the blessed company of all faithful people; that it may please God to confirm and strengthen it in purity of faith, in holiness of life, and in perfectness of love, and to restore to it the witness of visible unity; and more especially for that branch of the same planted by God in this land, whereof we are members; that in all things it may work according to God's will, serve him faithfully, and worship him acceptably.

You shall pray for the Leader of this Nation, and for the Governor of this State, and for all that are in authority; that all, and every one of them, may serve truly in their several callings to the glory of God, and the edifying and well-governing of the people, remembering the account they shall be called upon to give at the last great day.

You shall also pray for the ministers of God's Holy Word and Sacraments; for Bishops (and herein more especially for the Bishop of this Diocese), that they may minister faithfully and wisely the discipline of Christ; likewise for all Priests and Deacons (and herein more especially for the Clergy here residing), that they may shine as lights in the world, and in all things may adorn the doctrine of God our Savior.

And you shall pray for a due supply of persons fitted to serve God in the Ministry and in the State; and to that end, as well as for the good education of all the youth of this land, you shall pray for all schools, colleges, and seminaries of sound and godly learning, and for all whose hands are open for their maintenance; that whatsoever tends to the advancement of true religion and useful learning may for ever flourish and abound.

You shall pray for all the people of this Nation, that they may live in the true faith and fear of God, and in brotherly charity one towards another.

You shall pray also for all who travel by land, sea, air, or space; for all prisoners and captives; for all who are in sickness or in sorrow; for all who have fallen into grievous sin; for all who, through temptation, ignorance, helplessness, grief, trouble, dread, or the near approach of death, especially need our prayers.

You shall also praise God for rain and sunshine; for the fruits of the earth; for the products of all honest industry; and for all his good gifts, temporal and spiritual, to us and to all men.

Finally, you shall yield unto God most high praise and hearty thanks for the wonderful grace and virtue declared in all his saints, who have been the choice vessels of his grace and the lights of the world in their several generations; and pray unto God, that we may have grace to direct our lives after their good examples; that, this life ended, we may be made partakers with them of the glorious resurrection, and the life everlasting.

And now, brethren, summing up all our petitions, and all our thanksgivings, in the words which Christ hath taught us, we make bold to say,

Our Father, Who is in heaven, hallowed be Your Name. Your kingdom come, Your will be done, on earth, as it is in heaven. Give us this day, our daily bread, and forgive us our debts, as we forgive our debtors. And lead us not into temptation, but deliver us from evil. For Yours is the kingdom, and the power, and the glory, forever and ever. *Amen.*

BOOK OF ADDITIONAL SERVICES AND BLESSINGS

After Communion Thanksgiving Prayers

Let my mouth be filled with Your praise, O Lord, that I may sing of Your glory, for You have granted me to partake of Your holy, divine, immortal, and life-giving Mysteries. Keep me in Your holiness that I may meditate on Your justice all the day long. Alleluia. Alleluia. Alleluia.

Thanksgiving Prayer of St. Basil the Great

Lord Christ our God, King of the ages and Creator of all, I thank You for all the blessings You have granted me and for the communion of Your pure and life-giving Mysteries. I pray for You, therefore, good Lord and Lover of men, to guard me under Your protection and within the shadow of Your wings; and grant me with a clear conscience till my last breath worthily to partake of Your holy things for forgiveness of sins and for life eternal. For You are the Bread of Life, the Source of Holiness, the Giver of all that is good, and to You we give glory, with the Father and the Holy Spirit, now and forever. Amen.

Anonymous

I thank You, O Lord my God, that You have not rejected me, a sinner, but have granted me to be a communicant of Your holy things. I thank You that You have granted me, unworthy as I am, to partake of Your pure and heavenly gifts. But, O Lord, Lover of men, Who died for us and rose again and bestowed upon us these Your dread and life-giving Mysteries for the wellbeing and sanctification of our souls and bodies, grant that these may be even to me for the healing of my soul and body, for the averting of everything hostile, for the enlightenment of he eyes of my heart, for the peace of the powers of my souls, for unashamed faith, for sincere love, for the fullness of wisdom, for the keeping of Your commandments for an increase of Your divine grace, and for familiarity with Your kingdom; that being kept by them in Your holiness I may ever remember Your grace, and never live for myself but for You our Lord and Benefactor. And so, when I have passed from existence here in the hope of eternal life, may I attain to everlasting rest where the song is unceasing of those who keep festival and the joy is boundless of those who behold the ineffable beauty of Your face. For You are the true desire and the unutterable gladness of those who love You, O Christ our God, and all creation sings of You throughout the ages. Amen.

From John Knox's *Manner of the Administration of the Lord's Supper*

Most merciful Father, we offer to You all praise, thanks, and glory, that in Your great mercy, it has pleased You to grant us, who are miserable sinners, so excellent a gift and treasure, as to receive us into the fellowship and company of Your dear Son Jesus Christ our Lord. You delivered Him to death for us, and now You have given Him to us as food and nourishment for eternal life. And now we pray, O heavenly Father, that You will never permit us to become so ungrateful as to forget Your wonderful benefits; but impart and lock them in our hearts, so that we may grow and increase more and more in true faith each day, and that we may continually use our faith in all kinds of good work; and O Lord, make us strong in every difficulty so that we may constantly stand in the confession of faith, glorifying You in our lives, You Who are God over all things, and blessed forever. So be it. Amen.

From G.C. Binyon's *Prayers for the City of God*

O Christ, our only Savior, so live within us that we may go from here with the light of hope in our eyes, and the fire of inspiration on our lips, Your Word on our tongues, and Your love in our hearts. Amen.

Prayer of St. Thomas Aquinas

I thank You, O Holy Lord, Almighty Father, Eternal God, Who has deigned, not through any merits of mine, but out of the condescension of Your goodness, to satisfy me, a sinner, Your unworthy servant, with the precious Body and Blood of Your Son, our Lord Jesus Christ. I pray that this Holy Communion be not a condemnation to punishment for me, but a saving plea to forgiveness. May it be to me the armor of faith and the shield of a good will. May it be to the emptying out of my vices and the extinction of all lustful desires; and increase of charity and patience, of humility and obedience, and all virtues; a strong defense against the snares of all my enemies, visible and invisible; the perfect quieting of all my evil impulses of flesh and spirit, binding me firmly to You, the One True God; and a happy ending of my life. I pray, too, that You will deign to bring me, a sinner, to that ineffable banquet where

You, with Your Son and the Holy Spirit, are to Your Saints true Light, fulfillment of desires, eternal joy, unalloyed gladness, and perfect bliss. Through Jesus Christ our Lord. Amen.

Prayer Before Bible Study

O God of grace and mercy, I give you humble thanks for this time of studying your holy word. Teach me and speak to me. Open my heart and mind to comprehend. Grant me, Your servant, knowledge, wisdom, and understanding. Help me to grow and learn and become more like Christ, in Whose Holy Name I pray. Amen.

Blessing of Businesses

Blessed be God, who has begun a good work in us. Blessed be the name of the Lord.

All respond:

Now and forever.

The leader may use these or similar words to introduce the blessing:

Jesus showed us the dignity of labor. He was known as the carpenter's son, and he willingly worked with the tools of his trade. Through the labor of our hands, we bring God's blessing upon ourselves and others. Let us pray for all who do business and for those who will share the fruit of their labor.

Then the Scripture is read:

Psalm 23 A Psalm of David.
23 The LORD is my shepherd,
I will not be in need.
² He lets me lie down in green pastures;
He leads me beside quiet waters.

³ He restores my soul;
He guides me in the paths of righteousness
For the sake of His name.
⁴ Even though I walk through the valley of the shadow of death,
I fear no evil, for You are with me;
Your rod and Your staff, they comfort me.
⁵ You prepare a table before me in the presence of my enemies;
You have anointed my head with oil;
My cup overflows.
⁶ Certainly goodness and faithfulness will follow me all the days of my life,
And my dwelling *will be* in the house of the LORD forever.

Colossians 3.12-17

¹² So, as those who have been chosen of God, holy and beloved, put on a heart of compassion, kindness, humility,
gentleness, *and* patience; ¹³ bearing with one another, and forgiving each other, whoever has a complaint against anyone; just as the Lord forgave you, so *must* you *do* also. ¹⁴ In addition to all these things *put on* love, which is the perfect bond of unity. ¹⁵ Let the peace of Christ, to which you were indeed called in one body, rule in your hearts; and be thankful. ¹⁶ Let the word of Christ richly dwell within you, with all wisdom teaching and admonishing one another with psalms, hymns, *and* spiritual songs, singing with thankfulness in your hearts to God. ¹⁷ Whatever you do in word or deed, *do* everything in the name of the Lord Jesus, giving thanks through Him to God the Father.

The reader concludes:

The word of the Lord.

All respond:

Thanks be to God.

O God, in your wise providence, you are glad to bless all human labor, the work of our hands and of our minds. Grant that all here, who plan and conduct business may, through your guidance and support, come to right decisions and carry them out fairly. We ask this through Christ our Lord. Amen.

Almighty God, our heavenly Father, who declares Your glory and shows forth Your handiwork in the heavens and in the earth: Deliver, we beseech You, in our many different callings, from the service of mammon, that we may do the work which You give us to do, in truth, in beauty, and in righteousness, with singleness of heart as your servants, and to the benefit of our fellow men, for the sake of Him who came among us as one that serves, Your Son, Jesus Christ our Lord. Amen.

O God the Creator of all, Who blesses seed and increases it and makes it useful for our use: Be well pleased, out of Your own deep compassion, to bless + and sanctify these businesses. O God, you instructed us to use for our needs the fruit and work of these businesses and knowing how to do good through human labor, we pray to Your Majesty: Be pleased to + bless these businesses and increase them for the sake of the human race; + preserve them and cause them to prosper. Let everyone hoping in Your Majesty and the expanse of Your compassions, who are laboring in these businesses, be granted abundant fruit or their labors and to be filled with heavenly blessings, through Jesus Christ our Lord, to Whom be glory and honor forever. Amen.

Then <u>holy water shall be sprinkled</u> on all the participants.

All make the Sign of the Cross +, as the leader concludes:

May God, the Father of goodness, who commanded us to help one another as brothers and sisters, + bless these businesses with his presence and look kindly on all who labor there. Amen

And may almighty God bless you, + the Father, and + the Son, + and the Holy Spirit. Amen.

Blessing of a New Home

Priest: In the Name of the Father, and of the Son, and of the Holy Spirit. As it was in the beginning, is now, and ever shall be, world without end. Amen.

All: OUR Father, who are in heaven, hallowed be Your Name. Your kingdom come, Your will be done, on earth as it is in heaven. Give us this day our daily bread and forgive us our debts as we forgive our debtors. And lead us not into temptation, but deliver us from evil. For Yours is the kingdom and the power and the glory forever. Amen.

Priest: He who dwells in the shelter of the Most High will abide in the shadow of the Almighty.
I will say to the Lord, "My refuge and my fortress, my God, in whom I trust." (Psalm 91.1-2)

Priest. O God, be hasty to save us.
Answer. *O Lord, make haste to help us. (Psalm 70.1)*

Priest: Glory be to the Father, and to the Son, and to the Holy Spirit.
All: As it was in the beginning, is now, and ever shall be, world without end. Amen.

Alleluia!

Antiphon: My people will abide in a peaceful habitation, in secure dwellings, and in quiet resting places. (Isaiah 32.18)

Psalm 15

15 LORD, who may reside in Your tent?
Who may settle on Your holy hill?
² One who walks with integrity, practices righteousness,
And speaks truth in his heart.

3 He does not slander with his tongue,
Nor do evil to his neighbor,
Nor bring shame on his friend;
4 A despicable person is despised in his eyes,
But he honors those who fear the LORD;
He takes an oath to his own detriment, and does not change;
5 He does not lend his money at interest,
Nor does he take a bribe against the innocent.
One who does these things will never be shaken.

Priest: Glory be to the Father, and to the Son, and to the Holy Spirit.
All: As it was in the beginning, is now, and ever shall be, world without end. Amen.

Antiphon: My people will abide in a peaceful habitation, in secure dwellings, and in quiet resting places. (Isaiah 32.18)

Priest: Let us pray.
O Lord our God, we pray that You will enlighten this dwelling with Your lovingkindness, fill it with holy residents, and grant unto your servants living within the protection of Your Divine Majesty. Amen.

Priest: The Lord be with you.
All: And with your spirit.
Priest: Let us pray.

Priest: Lord have mercy upon us.
All: Christ have mercy upon us.
Priest: Lord have mercy upon us.

All: OUR Father, who are in heaven, hallowed be Your Name. Your kingdom come, Your will be done, on earth as it is in heaven. Give us this day our daily bread and forgive us our debts as we forgive our debtors. And lead us not into temptation, but deliver us from evil. For Yours is the kingdom and the power and the glory forever. Amen.

Priest: Hear my prayer, O Lord;
All: And let my cry come to you. (Psalm 102.1)
Priest: Let us pray.

The priest takes holy water and sprinkles each room, while saying the following prayer:

O Lord, we implore You to bless the goings out and the comings in of those who reside in this house; grant to keep them in purity and health; to send Your holy angel to be their defense; to drive away darkness and grant light; to give the enemy no advantage against them; to bestow on them a sufficient amount of food and clothing; to enrich them with the works of faith; and to surround them with the unity of the Blessed Trinity; through Jesus Christ our Lord. Amen.

And, with the Cross, making the sign of the Cross, he continues:

Let this house be + hallowed, and the unclean spirits be + driven from it through the might of our Lord Jesus Christ; and to those who reside within this house, grant + health, cheerfulness, and gladness and that they be guarded and preserved in them by Your Divine Majesty, O Almighty God; through Jesus Christ our Lord. Amen.

O Lord, our Heavenly Father, Almighty, Everlasting God, hear us, and grant that You will send Your holy angel to guard, cherish, protect, visit, and defend all who reside in this home. Through the might of our Lord Jesus Christ. Amen.

Almighty God + bless this house and the people in it, and as You blessed the house of Abraham, Isaac, and Jacob, so grant to + bless and hallow this house and all who live in it. Through our Lord Jesus Christ who lives and reigns with You and the Holy Spirit, now and forever. Amen.

Priest: The + blessing of God Almighty, the Father, the Son, and the Holy Spirit, be upon this house and all living within it. Amen.

Blessing of a Vehicle

Priest: Holy God the Father in heaven
Answer: Have mercy on us.
Priest: Holy God the Son, Redeemer of the world
Answer: Have mercy on us.
Priest: Holy God the Holy Spirit the Lord and Giver of Life
Answer: Have mercy on us.
Priest: O Most Holy Trinity three Persons and One God
Answer: Have mercy on us.
Priest: Glory to the Father, and to the Son, and to the Holy Spirit
Answer: As it was in the beginning, is now, and ever shall be, world without end. *Amen.*

The reading is Psalm 91.

91 One who dwells in the shelter of the Most High
Will lodge in the shadow of the Almighty.
2 I will say to the LORD, "My refuge and my fortress,
My God, in whom I trust!"
3 For it is He who rescues you from the net of the trapper
And from the deadly plague.
4 He will cover you with His pinions,
And under His wings you may take refuge;
His faithfulness is a shield and wall.
5 You will not be afraid of the terror by night,
Or of the arrow that flies by day;
6 Of the plague that stalks in darkness,
Or of the destruction that devastates at noon.
7 A thousand may fall at your side
And ten thousand at your right hand,
But it shall not approach you.
8 You will only look on with your eyes
And see the retaliation *against* the wicked.
9 For you have made the LORD, my refuge,

The Most High, your dwelling place.
¹⁰ No evil will happen to you,
Nor will any plague come near your tent.
¹¹ For He will give His angels orders concerning you,
To protect you in all your ways.
¹² On their hands they will lift you up,
So that you do not strike your foot against a stone.
¹³ You will walk upon the lion and cobra,
You will trample the young lion and the serpent.
¹⁴ "Because he has loved Me, I will save him;
I will set him *securely* on high, because he has known My name.
¹⁵ He will call upon Me, and I will answer him;
I will be with him in trouble;
I will rescue him and honor him.
¹⁶ I will satisfy him with a long life,
And show him My salvation."

Priest: O Lord our God, Who sits on the Seraphim and rides on the Cherubim, and Who has adorned men with wisdom out of the goodness of Your Providence, guiding all to good: send Your blessing on this vehicle and set Your angel on it that those traveling in it may be protected and directed in peace from all harm, evil intentions, wrecks, breakdowns, and anything that might harm them. And, O Lord, having successfully completed their journey, they may give glory and thanksgiving to You, praising the Father, the Son, and the Holy Spirit, ever One God. *Amen.*

Then the Priest anoints the vehicle with oil, or else sprinkles it with holy water inside and out, and then says:

Priest: Blessed and sanctified is this vehicle, in the Name of the Father, and of the Son, and of the Holy Spirit, ever one God, world without end. *Amen.*

OCCASIONAL SERVICES

Holy Communion for the Homebound and Infirm

(This service is for pre-consecrated Holy Communion. None should be left over after all who are to commune have done so, but any leftovers must be reverently consumed by the priest or deacon.)

OUR FATHER, Who is in heaven, hallowed be Your Name. Your kingdom come, Your will be done, on earth, as it is in heaven. Give us this day, our daily bread, and forgive us our debts, as we forgive our debtors. And lead us not into temptation, but deliver us from evil. For Yours is the kingdom, and the power, and the glory, forever and ever. *Amen.*
(Matthew 6:9-13)

Priest.   The Lord be with you.
Answer. And with your spirit.
Priest.   Let us pray.

ALMIGHTY GOD, all hearts are open to you. All desires are known to you, and from you no secrets are hidden. Cleanse the thoughts of our hearts by the inspiration of your Holy Spirit so that we may love you perfectly, and in a worthy manner magnify your Holy Name; through Christ our Lord. *Amen.*

Here may be read the PSALM for the day followed by the GOSPEL of the day, however the priest shall be mindful of the frailty and infirmity of those who are to commune and may skip this part.

Priest: Let us confess our sins to Almighty God.

ALMIGHTY God, Father of our Lord Jesus Christ, Maker of all things, Judge of all men. We acknowledge and deeply mourn our manifold sins and wickedness, Which we, from time to time, most grievously have committed, By thought, word, and deed, Against your Divine Majesty, Provoking most justly your wrath and indignation against us. We earnestly repent, And are greatly sorry for our wrongdoings. The remembrance of them is grievous unto us. The burden of them is

intolerable. Have mercy upon us, Have mercy upon us, most merciful Father. For your Son our Lord Jesus Christ's sake, Forgive us all that is past. And grant that from now on we may Serve and please you in newness of life, To the honor and glory of your Name; Through Jesus Christ our Lord. *Amen.*
(Romans 6.4; 2 Corinthians 1.19-20; James 5.19; 1 John 1.18-19)

Then the Priest (or the Bishop if he is present) shall say:

ALMIGHTY God, our heavenly Father, who of his great mercy has promised forgiveness of sins to all those who with genuine repentance and true faith turn to him; Have mercy upon you; + pardon and deliver you from all your sins; establish and strengthen you in all goodness; and bring you to everlasting life; through Jesus Christ our Lord. *Amen.*
(Matthew 16.19; Acts 13.38-39; John 20.23)

Then the Priest shall say:

Hear what comfortable words our Savior Christ says to all who truly turn to Him.

Come to Me, all who are weary and burdened, and I will give you rest. *St Matthew 11:28*
For God so loved the world, that He gave His only-begotten Son, that whoever believes in Him should not perish, but have everlasting life. *St John 3:16*

Offering Holy Communion, the priest says:

The Servant of God (name) receives the All-holy Body of our Lord, God, and Savior Jesus Christ.
The person is communed with the bread.

Then the priest says:

The Servant of God (name) receives the All-Holy Blood of our Lord, God, and Savior Jesus Christ.

Here may be said one of the Thanksgiving Prayers for after communion. Then the priest shall say:

Priest: THE peace of God, which passes all understanding, keep your hearts and minds in the knowledge and love of God, and of His Son Jesus Christ our Lord: And the blessing + of God Almighty, the Father, the Son, and the Holy Spirit, be among you and remain with you always. *Amen.*
(Ephesians 3.14-19; Colossians 2.2-3; Philippians 4.7)

The Office of Compline

Priest: Restore us again, O God of our salvation,
All: and put away your indignation toward us! (Psalm 85.4)

Priest: Be of sober *spirit,* be on the alert. Your adversary, the devil, prowls around like a roaring lion, seeking someone to devour. So resist him, firm in *your* faith, knowing that the same experiences of suffering are being accomplished by your brothers and sisters who are in the world. (1 St. Peter 5.8-9)

Priest: But You, O Lord, have mercy upon us.
People: Thanks be to God.
Priest: Our help stands in the name of the Lord.
People: Who has made heaven and earth.
(Psalm 123.3; 124.8)

ALL: ALMIGHTY and most merciful Father; We have erred, and strayed from Your ways like lost sheep. We have followed too much the plans and desires of our own hearts. We committed offense against Your holy laws. We have left undone those things which we ought to have done; And we have done those things which we ought not to have done; And there is no health in us. But You, O Lord, have mercy upon us, miserable offenders. Spare those, O God, who confess their faults. Restore those who are penitent; According to Your promises declared unto mankind in Christ Jesus our Lord. And grant, O most merciful

Father, for His sake; That from here onward we may live a godly, righteous, and sober life, To the glory of Your holy Name. *Amen.*

Priest: ALMIGHTY God, the Father of our Lord Jesus Christ, does not desire the death of a sinner, but rather that he may turn from his wickedness and live. He pardons and absolves all those who truly repent, and sincerely believe his holy Gospel.

Wherefore let us implore Him to grant us true repentance, and His Holy Spirit, that those things may please Him that we do at this present time; and that the rest of our life hereafter may be pure and holy; so that at the last we may come to His eternal joy; through Jesus Christ our Lord.

(If there is no priest, the leader says: Merciful Lord, grant us forgiveness of all our sins, true repentance, and renewal of life, and the grace and comfort of your Holy Spirit. *Amen. (Luke 1.77))*

Stand

Priest: In your righteousness deliver and rescue us;
All: Incline your ear to us and save us.
(Psalm 135.2)

Priest: Glory to the Father, and to the Son, and to the Holy Spirit.
All: As it was in the beginning, is now, and ever shall be, world without end. Amen.

During the Year:	**During Eastertide:**
Priest: Praise the Lord.	Priest: Alleluia!
All: The Lord's Name be praised.	All: Alleluia!
(Psalm 135.1)	

Priest: The Lord Almighty grant us a peaceful night and a perfect end. Amen. (Romans 15.33; Matthew 25.23)

ONE *of the following Psalms shall be read, excepting one from either Morning Prayer or Evening Prayer may be substituted.*

Sit

Psalm 4

4 Answer me when I call, God of my righteousness!
You have relieved me in my distress;
Be gracious to me and hear my prayer.
2 You sons of man, how long will my honor be *treated as* an insult?
How long will you love what is worthless and strive for a lie? *Selah*
3 But know that the LORD has set apart the godly person for Himself;
The LORD hears when I call to Him.
4 Tremble, and do not sin;
Meditate in your heart upon your bed, and be still. *Selah*
5 Offer the sacrifices of righteousness,
And trust in the LORD.
6 Many are saying, "Who will show us *anything* good?"
Lift up the light of Your face upon us, LORD!
7 You have put joy in my heart,
More than when their grain and new wine are abundant.
8 In peace I will both lie down and sleep,
For You alone, LORD, have me dwell in safety.

Priest: Glory to the Father, and to the Son, and to the Holy Spirit.
All: As it was in the beginning, is now, and ever shall be, world without
end. Amen.

Or

Psalm 31.1-5

31 In You, LORD, I have taken refuge;
Let me never be put to shame;
In Your righteousness rescue me.
2 Incline Your ear to me, rescue me quickly;
Be a rock of strength for me,
A stronghold to save me.
3 For You are my rock and my fortress;
For the sake of Your name You will lead me and guide me.
4 You will pull me out of the net which they have secretly laid for me,
For You are my strength.

⁵ Into Your hand I entrust my spirit;
You have redeemed me, LORD, God of truth.

Priest: Glory to the Father, and to the Son, and to the Holy Spirit.
All: As it was in the beginning, is now, and ever shall be, world without
end. Amen.

Or

Psalm 91

91 One who dwells in the shelter of the Most High
Will lodge in the shadow of the Almighty.
² I will say to the LORD, "My refuge and my fortress,
My God, in whom I trust!"
³ For it is He who rescues you from the net of the trapper
And from the deadly plague.
⁴ He will cover you with His pinions,
And under His wings you may take refuge;
His faithfulness is a shield and wall.
⁵ You will not be afraid of the terror by night,
Or of the arrow that flies by day;
⁶ Of the plague that stalks in darkness,
Or of the destruction that devastates at noon.
⁷ A thousand may fall at your side
And ten thousand at your right hand,
But it shall not approach you.
⁸ You will only look on with your eyes
And see the retaliation *against* the wicked.
⁹ For you have made the LORD, my refuge,
The Most High, your dwelling place.
¹⁰ No evil will happen to you,
Nor will any plague come near your tent.
¹¹ For He will give His angels orders concerning you,
To protect you in all your ways.
¹² On their hands they will lift you up,
So that you do not strike your foot against a stone.
¹³ You will walk upon the lion and cobra,
You will trample the young lion and the serpent.

¹⁴ "Because he has loved Me, I will save him;
I will set him *securely* on high, because he has known My name.
¹⁵ He will call upon Me, and I will answer him;
I will be with him in trouble;
I will rescue him and honor him.
¹⁶ I will satisfy him with a long life,
And show him My salvation."

Priest: Glory to the Father, and to the Son, and to the Holy Spirit.
All: As it was in the beginning, is now, and ever shall be, world without
end. Amen.

Or

Psalm 134

134 Behold, bless the LORD, all you servants of the LORD,
Who serve by night in the house of the LORD!
² Lift up your hands to the sanctuary
And bless the LORD.
³ May the LORD bless you from Zion,
He who made heaven and earth.

Priest: Glory to the Father, and to the Son, and to the Holy Spirit.
All: As it was in the beginning, is now, and ever shall be, world without
end. Amen.

*Read ONE of the following verses of Scripture, or substitute one from the
daily readings.*

Yet You are in our midst, LORD, and we are called by Your name; Do
not leave us!"
Jeremiah 14.9

Come to Me, all who are weary and burdened, and I will give you
rest. Take My yoke upon you and learn from Me, for I am gentle and
humble in heart, and YOU WILL FIND REST FOR YOUR SOULS. For My yoke
is comfortable, and My burden is light.
St. Matthew 11.28-30

Now may the God of peace, who brought up from the dead the great
Shepherd of the sheep through the blood of the eternal covenant, *that
is,* Jesus our Lord, equip you in every good thing to do His
will, working in us that which is pleasing in His sight, through Jesus
Christ, to whom *be* the glory forever and ever. Amen.
Hebrews 13.20-21

Now shall be said or sung one *of the following hymns:*

ALL:
1] The day is past and over;
all thanks, O Lord, to thee!
I pray thee now that sinless
the hours of dark may be.
O Jesus, keep me in thy sight,
and guard me through the
coming night.

2] The joys of day are over;
I lift my heart to thee,
and ask thee that offenseless
the hours of dark may be.
O Jesus, keep me in thy sight,
and guard me through the
coming night.

3] The toils of day are over;
I raise the hymn to thee,
and ask that free from peril
the hours of dark may be.
O Jesus, keep me in thy sight,
and guard me through the
coming night.

4] Be thou my soul's preserver,
for thou alone dost know
how many are the perils
through which I have to go.
O loving Jesus, hear my call,
and guard and save me from
them all.

Or this hymn

ALL:
1] To You before the close of day,
Creator of the world, we pray,
That, with You gracious favour
endow
Would be our guard and keeper now.

2] From all ill dreams defend our
sight,
From fears and terrors of the night,
Withhold from us our spiritual foe,

3] O Father, that we ask be
done,
Through Jesus Christ, Your
only Son,
Who, with the Spirit
blessedly
living and reigning eternally.

That spot of sin we may not know.

Priest: Into Your hands I commit my spirit;
All: You have redeemed me faithful God. (Psalm 31.5)
Priest: Keep me as the apple of Your eye;
All: Hide me in the shadow of Your wings. (Psalm 17.8)

Priest: Save us O Lord, watching, guard us sleeping,
All: that we may watch with Christ, and rest in peace.

Priest: Lord, now let Your servant depart in peace, according to Your word, for mine eyes have seen Your salvation which You have prepared in the presence of all peoples, to be a light of revelation to the Gentiles, and the glory of Your people Israel.

Priest: Save us O Lord, watching, guard us sleeping,
All: that we may watch with Christ, and rest in peace.

Priest: Let us confess our faith together.

All: I BELIEVE in God the Father Almighty, Maker of heaven and earth:
     And in Jesus Christ his only Son our Lord; Who was conceived by the Holy Spirit, Born of the Virgin Mary; Suffered under Pontius Pilate, Was crucified, dead, and buried; He descended into hell; The third day he rose again from the dead; He ascended into heaven, And sits on the right hand of God the Father Almighty; From there he shall come to judge the living and the dead.
     I believe in the Holy Spirit; The holy Catholic* Church; The Communion of Saints; The Forgiveness of sins, The Resurrection of the body; And the Life everlasting. *Amen.*

Priest: Lord have mercy upon us.
All: Christ have mercy upon us.
Priest: Lord have mercy upon us.

All: Our Father Who is in heaven, hallowed be Your Name. Your kingdom come, Your will be done, on earth, as it is in heaven. Give us this day our daily bread, and forgive us our debts, as we forgive our debtors; and lead us not into temptation, but deliver us from evil. For Yours is the kingdom and the power and the glory, forever. Amen.

Priest: Let us pray.
Priest: Lord, lighten our darkness and in Your great mercy, defend us from all perils and dangers of this night; for the love of Your Only-Begotten Son, our Savior Jesus Christ. Amen.
(Psalm 18.28; 91.5; Isaiah 42.16; 50.10; Micah 7.8; John 1.5; 8.12; Ephesians 5.8)

Merciful God, be present and protect us through the quiet hours of this night, so that we, wearied by the changes and uncertainty of this passing world may rest in the knowledge that Your Son Jesus Christ is the same yesterday, today, and forever; through our only Mediator and Advocate, Jesus Christ our Lord. Amen.
(1 Thessalonians 5.6; Hebrews 13.8)

Lord, visit this place and drive away all the snares of the enemy; let your holy angels be present to preserve us in peace, and may your blessing be upon us always; through Jesus Christ our Lord. Amen.
(Psalm 141.9; 91.11)

Priest: In peace I will lie down and sleep;
All: for You alone, O Lord, make me dwell in safety.
(Psalm 4.8)

Priest: Let us bless the Lord;
All: Thanks be to God.
(Revelation 7.12)

Priest: The Lord Almighty grant us a peaceful night and a perfect end. Amen.
(Romans 15.33; Matthew 25.23)

Priest: The Almighty and merciful Lord, Father, Son, and Holy Spirit, bless us and keep us. Amen.
(Numbers 6.24)

THANKSGIVINGS

To be used after the General Thanksgiving, or, when that is not said, before the final Prayer of Blessing or the Benediction.

A Thanksgiving to Almighty God for the Fruits of the Earth and all the other Blessings of his merciful Providence

MOST gracious God, by whose knowledge the depths are broken up, and the clouds drop down the dew: we yield You genuine thanks and praise for the return of seed-time and harvest, for the increase of the ground and the gathering in of the fruits thereof, and for all the other blessings of Your merciful providence bestowed upon this nation and people. And, we entreat You, give us a just sense of these great mercies; such as may appear in our lives by an humble, holy, and obedient walking before You all our days; through Jesus Christ our Lord, to whom, with You and the Holy Spirit, be all glory and honor, world without end. *Amen.*

A Thanksgiving Day Prayer

O God, our true life, in whom and by whom all things live, we, your thankful and unworthy servants, praise and glorify you, O Lord, for your great benefits which we have received; we bless you, we thank you, and magnify your great goodness. The eyes of all wait upon you, Good Lord, and you give them their food in due season. You open your hand and fill all living things with your plenteousness. You make springs pour water into the ravines; it flows between the mountains. They give water to all the beasts of the field; the wild donkeys quench their thirst. The birds of the air nest by the waters; they sing among the branches. You water the mountains from your upper chambers; the earth is satisfied by the fruit of your work. You make grass grow for the cattle, and plants for man to cultivate— bringing forth food from the earth: wine that gladdens the heart of man, oil to make his face shine, and bread that sustains his heart. The trees of the LORD are well watered, the trees that you planted. There the birds make their nests; the stork has its home in the pine trees. The high mountains belong to the wild goats; the crags are a refuge for the rock badgers. To these blessings, O Lord, we add our heartfelt thanks for all your mercies; for our lives, our reason, and all other endowments and faculties of soul and body; for our health, family members, friends, food, raiment, and all the other comforts and conveniences of life. Above all we adore your mercy in sending your Only-Begotten Son into the world, to redeem us from sin and eternal death, and in giving us the knowledge and sense of our responsibility towards you. We bless you for your patience with us, notwithstanding our many provocations; for all the directions, assistances, and comforts of your Holy Spirit; for your continual care and watchful providence over us through the whole course of our lives; and particularly for the mercies and benefits of this present day, beseeching you to continue these blessings to us, and to give us grace to show our thankfulness in a sincere obedience to your laws, for through the merits and intercessions of your Son Jesus Christ we have received them all.

Therefore, look down our One True God, Three yet One, on the food of your servants and sanctify it, as you sanctified the ram which faithful Abraham brought to you, and the lamb which Able offered to you as a whole offering. Likewise the fatted calf which you commanded to be slain for your Prodigal Son when he was granted to enjoy your grace and be filled with healthful food, and as you blessed the loaves and fishes with your precious holy hands for the nourishment and strengthening of your creatures, so too may we enjoy these things sanctified and blessed by you for the nourishment of us all. For you are the True Nourishment and the Bestower of every good bounty and thing. Therefore, we, your humble servants offer you thanksgiving, praise, and glory through our Lord Jesus Christ. Amen.

The Thanksgiving of Women after Child-birth

To be said when any, Woman, being present in Church, shall have desired to return thanks to Almighty God for her safe deliverance.

O ALMIGHTY God, we give You humble thanks that You have been graciously pleased to preserve, through the great pain and peril of childbirth, this woman, Your servant, who desires now to offer her praises and thanksgivings unto You. Most Merciful Father, we ask You to grant that she, through Your help, may both faithfully live and walk according to Your will in this present life and also may be partaker of everlasting glory in the life to come; through Jesus Christ our Lord. *Amen.*

For Rain

O GOD, our heavenly Father, by whose gracious providence the earlier and the later rains descend upon the earth, that they may bring forth fruit for the use of man: we give You humble thanks that it has pleased You to send us rain to our great comfort, and to the glory of Your holy Name; through Jesus Christ our Lord. *Amen.*

For Fair Weather

O LORD God, who has justly humbled us by Your late visitation of us with immoderate rain and waters, and in Your mercy has relieved and comforted our souls by this seasonable and blessed change of weather; We praise and glorify Your holy Name for this Your mercy, and will always declare Your lovingkindness from generation to generation; through Jesus Christ our Lord. *Amen.*

For Plenty

O MOST merciful Father, who of Your gracious goodness has heard the devout prayers of Your Church, and turned our dearth and scarcity into plenty: we give You humble thanks for this Your special bounty; asking

You to continue Your lovingkindness unto us, that our land may yield us the fruits of its increase, to Your glory and our comfort; through Jesus Christ our Lord. *Amen.*

For Peace, and Deliverance from our Enemies

O ALMIGHTY God, who are a strong tower of defense unto Your servants against the face of their enemies: we yield You praise and thanksgiving for our deliverance from those great and apparent dangers wherewith we were surrounded. We acknowledge it was Your goodness that we were not delivered over as a prey unto them; entreating You still to continue such Your mercies towards us, that all the world may know that You are our Savior and mighty Deliverer; through Jesus Christ our Lord. *Amen.*

For Restoring Public Peace at Home

O ETERNAL God, our heavenly Father, who alone makes men to be of one mind in a house, and stills the outrage of a violent and unruly people: we bless Your holy Name, that it has pleased You to appease the seditious tumults which have been lately raised up amongst us; most humbly praying for You to grant to all of us grace, that we may henceforth obediently walk in Your holy commandments; and, leading a quiet and peaceable life in all godliness and honesty, may continually offer unto You our sacrifice of praise and thanksgiving for these Your mercies towards us; through Jesus Christ our Lord. *Amen.*

For Recovery from Sickness

O GOD, who are the giver of life, of health, and of safety: we bless Your Name, that You have been pleased to deliver from his bodily sickness this Your servant, who now desires to return thanks unto You, in the presence of all Your people. Gracious are You, O Lord, and full of compassion to the children of men. May his heart be duly impressed with a sense of Your merciful goodness, and may he devote the remainder of his days to an humble, holy, and obedient walking before You; through Jesus Christ our Lord. *Amen.*

For a Child's Recovery from Sickness

ALMIGHTY God and heavenly Father, we give You humble thanks for that You have been graciously pleased to deliver from his bodily sickness the child in whose behalf we bless and praise Your Name, in the presence of all Your people. We ask You to grant, O gracious Father, that he, through Your help, may both faithfully live in this world according to Your will, and also may be partaker of everlasting glory in the life to come; through Jesus Christ our Lord. *Amen.*

For a Safe Return from a Journey

MOST gracious Lord, whose mercy is over all Your works: we praise Your holy Name that You have been pleased to conduct in safety, through the perils of the great deep, the way of this Your servant, who now desires to return thanks unto You in Your holy Church. May he be duly sensible of Your merciful providence towards him, and ever express his thankfulness by a holy trust in You, and obedience to Your laws; through Jesus Christ our Lord. *Amen.*

Prayer for Missions

O Christ our True God, you have ordained that all of your people shall be a royal priesthood and bring the knowledge of your salvation to all nations. You are the only True God and only Way to the Father. We live in heathen lands among heathen people that know you not. Grant that through us the people in this nation will see you, O gracious Lord, for they live in abject darkness, with lives filled full of sin and despair. O Beautiful Savior, open the eyes of the people around us that they may see your beauty. Open their ears that they may hear your words of life that are like honey. Open their hearts to receive you as their most precious treasure. Grant them true repentance. Stay the darkness that oppresses them. Hold back the hand of the Enemy of our souls. Destroy the works of the devil and all false gods. Rise from your glorious righteous Throne and extend your mighty hand to save, and to heal, and to forgive. Let all of the nations rejoice and sing with one accord, "The Lord is Savior and apart from Jesus Christ there is none else." This we ask in your most holy and awesome name. Amen.

Prayer for a Childless (Heterosexual) Couple

Hear us, O Merciful and All-powerful God, that this petition be fulfilled by Your Grace. Be merciful, O Lord, to our supplications and remember your statute, by which You ordained the increase of the human race. Mercifully visit us, that this union which is in You, be preserved by Your helf. O Truly-gracious God, by Your power You made all things from nothingness, and established a beginning for all things; You make man in the Image of God with the inseparable help of woman; You have ordained that the body of woman conceive with the help of a man, and You taught us that what God has joined together ought never to be sundered. O our God, You sanctified the union of spouses with a high mystery in which was prefigured the mystical union of Christ with Your Church. The bride is joined to the husband and the first friendship is given a new arrangement with a blessing. Look down, O Merciful One, on these Your servants, (Names), who are joined together in marriage, and who entreat of You refuge and help, that there be in them such mercy, peace, and joy, that no deed of Satan may be found in them. Let them be fruitful, and let them see their children's children, granting them even third and fourth generations. And let them attain to ripe old age and enter into the heavenly tabernacle. For You are a Merciful God, and the Lover of mankind, and to You we give glory: To the Father, and to the Son, and to the Holy Spirit, now and forever. Amen.

Bishop's Prayers

The Blessing of the Oils and Consecration of the Holy Chrism

A Bishop may consecrate Holy Chrism and other Holy Oils as the needs arises. However, normally this is to be done on Maundy Thursday of each year. He is to consecrate enough oil for his diocese.

He shall celebrate the Holy Eucharist, being fully vested, and after the oblation of the Bread and Wine, at the end of the Church Militant prayer, the Archdeacon/Archpriest or other priests shall present to him the vessel containing the oil for the sick (which shall normally be brought into the sacristy by one of the assistant ministers or deacons attended by two altar servers). The assistant ministers or deacons shall say, "Reverend Father in God, the Oil for the Sick." The Bishop shall place the vessel at the Epistle corner of the Altar and shall say:

Bishop: The Lord be with you.
Response: And with your spirit.
Bishop: Let us pray.

Send, O Lord, we beseech You, Your Holy Spirit the Comforter from heaven upon this fatness of the olive, which You have granted to bring forth from the green tree, for the refreshment of body and soul; that as You did anoint Your priests, Kings, Prophets, and Martyrs, so this oil may, by Your blessing +, be to everyone anointed therewith, a heavenly medicine and remedy, to banish all pain, weakness, and suffering of body and soul, and that Your perfect anointing and blessing may abide within us for evermore. In the Name of our Lord Jesus Christ, who lives and reigns with You and the Holy Spirit, ever One God. Amen.

Let us pray.

O Lord Jesus Christ, whose name is as ointment poured forth in grace, purifying the world, Bless + and sanctify + this holy oil, the sigh of Your mercy, and impart it unto Your servants for salvation and deliverance from sickness; wash and cleanse the defilements of their souls, purge them from their manifold offences, assuage their sorrows, drive away their troubles, and scatter their afflictions. Through Your mercy we ask in your most awesome Name. Amen.

Then shall the Bishop deliver the Oil for the sick to the Archdeacon/Archpriest, who shall cause it to be carried to the sacristy.

Then shall the Oil for the Catechumens be brought in the same manner to the Bishop, who shall say:

Bishop: The Lord be with you.
Response: And with your spirit.
Bishop: Let us pray.

O God, Bestower of all spiritual increase and progress, Who by the might of Your Holy Spirit confirms the first efforts of feeble souls, we pray to You, O Lord, that you would grant to send Your blessing + upon this oil, and grant through its anointing cleansing of body and soul to them who shall come to the laver of blessed regeneration; that if any stains of their spiritual enemies have clung to them, they shall depart at the touch of this hallowed oil. Let there remain in them no room for spiritual wickedness, no abode for the rebel powers, no lurking-place for secret sins; but as Your servants come to the true faith, and to be cleansed by the operation of Your Holy Spirit, let this unction be profitable for that salvation which they are to obtain through the birth of heavenly regeneration in the Sacrament of Baptism. Through Jesus Christ our Lord, who lives and reigns with You and the Holy Spirit, ever One God, forever. Amen.

Then shall the Oil of the Catechumens be carried into the sacristy, and the Celebration shall proceed to the end of the preface and sanctus.

The Balsam and Oil for the Holy Chrism then be carried in two separate vessels by two Priests to the Archdeacon/Archpriest, while a third Priest bears the vessel in which they are to be mingled.

While this is being done, the choir sings:

Procession with the Oils to Be Blessed (no. 17)

O Redemptor

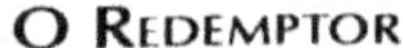

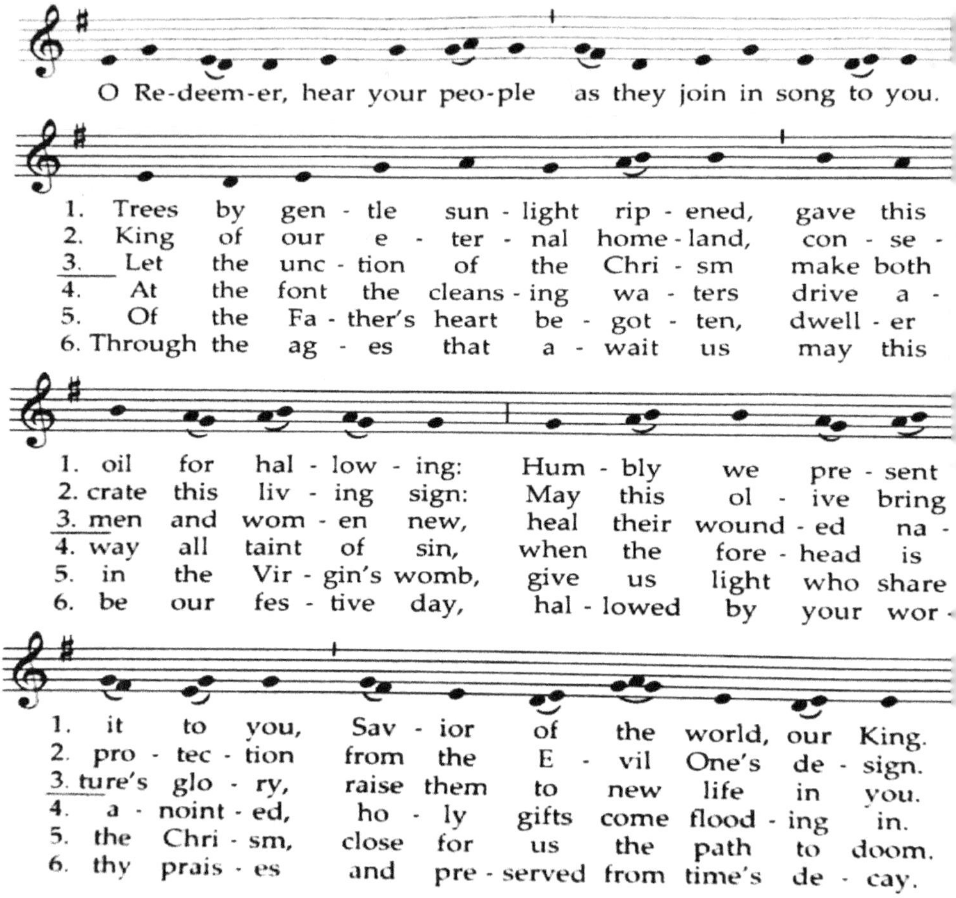

Then the Bishop shall pray as follows for the essential oils or perfumed oils:

Bishop: Let us pray to the Lord.

O God, Who ordains heavenly mysteries and powers, hear our prayers, we beseech You and grant that this fragrant oil, the sweet produce of Your Creation, which enriches us with priestly anointing, may be acceptable for Your service, and be hallowed + with Your blessing. Through Jesus Christ our Lord. Amen.

Let us Pray.

O Lord, maker of all creatures, Who by Your servant Moses commanded holy ointment to be compounded of principal spices, we humbly beseech Your mercy that You would bestow spiritual grace on this ointment, the fruit of a tree, and pour upon it the fullness of Your hallowing +. Let it be compounded for us, O Lord, with the gladness of faith, let it be the lasting Chrism of priestly anointing, let it be fitted for impressing the sign of the heavenly banner, that whoso are anointed therewith after being born again in Holy Baptism may obtain the fullest blessing of body and soul, and ever increase in the gift of that blessed faith which they have acquired. Through Jesus Christ our Lord, who lives and reigns with You and the Holy Spirit, ever One God. Amen.

Then the Bishop shall bless the Chrismal Oil as follows:

Be present, O Father Most Highest, and hearken to the prayers of us miserable sinners who call upon You. Send us, O Lord, the Holy Spirit wherewith You anointed Your Son above His fellows, that You may hallow + with the savour of Your ointments this Chrism here made ready and fulfill it with Your sevenfold spiritual graces. So grant to shine on them whom You redeem by spiritual washing, that this holy anointing may be to them the Chrism of blessing, the wedding garment, the bestowal of steadfastness, the remission of sins, the adoption of children, the increase of holy might, and the full perfection of spiritual grace; that whoso shall be signed with this holy anointing, and receive the Sacrament of the Body and Blood of Your dear Son Jesus Chirst, may feel Your protection, and obtain everlasting life. Through the same our Lord Jesus Christ, who lives and reigns with You and the same Spirit, ever one God, world without end. *Amen.*

Then mingling the fragrant oils and the Chrism Oil together, the Bishop shall pray:

In the Name of the Father + and of the Son + and of the Holy Spirit +, let this mingling be unto all anointed therewith for a propitiation and spiritual safeguard forever and ever. Amen.

Let us pray.

O God, Who among other gifts of Your bounty and lovingkindness has given the wholesome fruit of the olive for the use of man, and for the making of Holy Chrism; Who typified by that olive leaf which the dove brought back to the Ark when the waters abated, the remission of sins in Holy Baptism and the purifying unction of oil; Who commanded Your servant Moses that his brother Aaron should be anointed therewith for the priesthood of the Old Testament; Who bestowed on it yet greater honor, when Your Son Jesus Christ our Lord caused Himself to be baptized by John in the waters of Jordan, and You sent the Holy Spirit upon Him in the form of a Dove, declaring Him to be your Only-Begotten Son, in Whom You are well pleased, and showing thereby that You had anointed Him with the oil of gladness above His fellows, as David Your prophet testified, we pray You, O Lord, our heavenly Father, Almighty, everlasting God, though Your same Son our Lord Jesus Christ, that You would hallow + this matter of holy oil and fragrant oils sanctifying it + with the power of Your Anointed. And we humbly beg You, O Lord, that You would enrich this fatness with the might of the Holy Spirit, and make it abound with the sweetness of Divine Love, and establishing it with all blessing +. Let it be a holy unction and a sweet savour unto You, a sign of certain victory to those who are born again of water and the Holy Spirit, a joyful anointing, a hope of blessedness, a cleansing from sin, a medicine of life, and a help on their way to the heavenly country; that being sanctified in soul and body, they may be acknowledged by angels and archangels and all the heavenly powers, be feared by all evil and unclean spirits, and become a chosen generation, a royal priesthood, an holy nation, sealed with Your divine mystery, bearing Your Christ in their hearts, made a proper dwelling for You, O God the Father, through the grace of Your Holy Spirit and Your Adorable Son, Who live and reign with You in the Holy Trinity of co-eternal majesty, One God Almighty, world without end. Amen.

Then shall the Chrism be reverently carried to the Sacristy, and the Bishop shall proceed with the Holy Eucharist in the usual manner, ending with the blessing.

Bishop's Prayers for Various Occasions

BENEDICTION OF LITTLE CHILDREN

Bishop: Our help is in the Name of the Lord.
Response: Who has made heaven and earth.
Bishop: The Lord be with you.
Response: And with your spirit.
Bishop: Let us pray.

O Lord Jesus Christ, Who took into Your arms little children presented and coming unto You, and laying Your hands upon them (*here the Bishop shall lay his hands on the child's head*) and blessed them saying, Suffer the little children to come unto Me, and forbid them not, for of such is the kingdom of heaven, and their angels do ever behold the face of My Father; Have regard, we pray, unto the innocence of tis present infant, and the devotion of his (*her*) parents, and mercifully bless + him (*her*) by my ministry, that he (*she*) ever advancing by Your grace and mercy, may know You, love You, and fear You, may keep Your commandments and those of his (*her*) parents, and happily attain everlasting life. Through Your mercy.

The Blessing of God the Father + Almighty, of the Son +, and of the Holy Spirit +, descend upon you, keep you, govern you, and abide with you evermore. This we pray in Your most Awesome Name of the Father and of the Son and of the Holy Spirit. Amen.

PRIVATE PRAYERS FOR BISHOPS

For wisdom ruling

O Lord Jesus Christ, Shepherd and Bishop of souls, grant me to take the oversight of the flock committed to my charge, not as lording it over God's heritage, but in the spirit of servitude, wisdom and justice, of love and gentleness, that guiding Your sheep with You staff and rod I may at length enter with them into Your everlasting pastures. Through Your mercy in Jesus Christ our Lord. Amen.

For wise choice of Candidates for Holy Orders

O GOD, Who guided the lot which fell upon Your servant Matthias, grant me the gift of spiritual insight and discernment, that I may lay hands suddenly on no man, but choose for the ministry of Your Altar and the preaching of Your Word faithful men, who shall be an example to the flock in all godliness, and that no wolf may, by reason of my error or blindness, enter in to ravage and destroy the sheep which You have purchased with the Blood of Your dear Son. Through the same our Lord Jesus Christ, to whom with You and the Holy Spirit be all honour and glory, world without end. Amen.

For Simplicity of Life

O LORD JESUS CHRIST, King of kings, Whose earthly crown was of thorns, Whose sceptre was a reed, give me grace to shun all worldly pomp and luxury, and so to endure hardship as Your good soldier, that I may at length attain the spiritual riches of Your eternal Kingdom. Through Your mercy which is everlasting. Amen.

For right exercise of patronage

Grant, O Lord, that I may bestow the offices which You have entrusted to my stewardship on fit and worthy persons, choosing in all purity and simplicity of heart, not by favour or for my private advantage, lest I fall into condemnation for wasting Your goods, but solely for Your glory and the good of Your people. Through the Name of our Lord Jesus Christ. Amen.

Against Nepotism

O God, Who sent Your judgments upon Eli, and took the High Priesthood from his house by reason of his guilt in passing over the wickedness of his sons, preserve me, in Thy mercy, from falling into the like sin, and grant that I may never prefer the advantage of my kindred to the claims of Justice or the good of Your flock. Through Jesus Christ our Lord. Amen.

Before commencing any action against a Cleric

Take from me, O Lord, I beseech You, the spirit of anger and strife, grant me the spirit of peace and righteousness, that I may not enter upon this action with any thought of malice or revenge, nor rend thereby Your seamless robe but solely that just cause of scandal may be taken away from before Your people, and that the godly discipline of thy Church may be enforced. Through Jesus Christ our Lord. Amen.

For moral courage

Make me, O LORD, I pray, as a defenced city, and an iron pillar, on behalf of Your truth against the whole land, that I swerve not, like Pilate, from the right in order to content the people, but that righteousness may be the girdle of my loins, and faithfulness the girdle of my reins. Through Jesus Christ our Lord. Amen.

For zeal in reforms

O LORD JESU CHRIST, Who confirmed the covenant of peace and the High Priesthood to Your servant Phinehas, because he was zealous for his God, and Who did Yourself drive out from Your temple with a scourge of cords them who defiled it; fill me with such zeal for Your house that, fearing no man, and jealous for Your honour only, I may labour to cleanse and purge Your sanctuary from all offence, and so to purify Your priests and Levites as gold and silver, that they may offer the LORD an offering in righteousness. Through Jesus Christ our Lord. Amen.

For a supply of Candidates for Holy Orders

O GOD, Who has taught us in the Gospel to pray unto the LORD of the harvest to send faithful labourers into His harvest, since the harvest is great and the labourers but few; we humbly beseech You to send forth in Your Church such preachers of the Word as, enlightened by the Spirit of Wisdom, will steadfastly seek after Your glory, not their own honour, the salvation of souls, not their own advantage, and will be stewards of Your Word and of all that agrees therewith, in its true, salutary, and Apostolic sense and meaning. Through Jesus Christ our Lord. Amen.

For the Clergy

Hear our prayers, O LORD, and send the spirit of Your blessing upon Your servants the priests of this diocese, that enriched with heavenly gifts, they may both acquire Your Divine grace, and present to others an example of a godly life. Through Jesus Christ our Lord. Amen.

For the Metropolitan or Archbishop

O GOD, Shepherd and Ruler of all the faithful, mercifully look upon Your servant N., whom You have willed to govern Your Church; grant him, we entreat You, to be profitable in precept and example to those set under him, that he may, together with the flock entrusted to him, attain everlasting life. Through Jesus Christ our Lord. Amen.

For Peace in the Church

O GOD, bestower of peace, and lover of charity, grant Your servants true harmony with Your will, that we may be delivered from all temptations which beset us. Through Jesus Christ our Lord. Amen.

Against Persecutors of the Church

Almighty, everlasting GOD, show forth again the wonderful works of Your arm, as in olden times for the protection of the faithful, that our enemies may be subdued by Your power, and we may serve You with

Catholic faith and Christian devotion. Through Jesus Christ our Lord.
Amen.

O GOD, lover and keeper of peace and charity, grant to all our enemies
true peace and charity, grant them repentance and then remission of all
their sins, and mightily deliver us from all their snares. Through Jesus
Christ our Lord. Amen.

For True Faith and Holiness

O Heavenly FATHER, Almighty, everlasting, and merciful GOD, I beg
You to bestow on me true, sound, and Christian faith, sincere and
incorrupt, neither entangled in the meshes of error, nor spotted with
the stain of self-will.

Grant that my actions may so agree and correspond with my faith, that
it may not be defiled by any evil doings, lest I should seem to deny You
by an unholy life Whom I confess with a true faith.

Grant, O merciful Father, that I may serve You with good resolution
and ready will, that I may fulfill the works of righteousness, love mercy
and truth, shun all falsehood, think and speak no vain nor lying things,
but fear, love, and worship, You only, and keep Your commandments.

Grant me this grace also, that I may follow after and acknowledge none
other things than those which Your Holy Church, strengthened by the
Spirit of truth, teaches and confesses, until such time as I come unto
You in Thy Kingdom. Through Your most Holy Name, of the Father
and of the Son and of the Holy Spirit. Amen.

For grace to rule well.

Almighty, everlasting GOD, behold and see by what awful perils I am
beset on every side, by reason of the office which I discharge. I know
that it is for me no lordship, but a service and duty. I know that it is

not irrational creatures You have committed to my charge, but Your most chosen children, united to You by so close a bond of love that for them You did not hesitate to give Yourself unto death. Who am I , O my GOD to fulfil such a task. A weak and feeble man, prone to err and to be deceived. Your people are very great, and how can I be at hand in every place? Wherefore, O LORD, I humbly ask You, give me wisdom that sits by Your throne, send her out of Your holy heavens, and from the throne of Your glory, that being present she may labour with me, that I may know what is pleasing unto You, lest I should do aught through favour or hatred of any one, but may rather give my voice according to truth and righteousness. Through Jesus Christ our Lord, who with the Father and the Holy Spirit, ever One God, reigns forever. Amen.

For Diocesan Schools

Grant, O LORD, that we may not only ourselves abide in Your Word and doctrine, but bring up our children also for the glory of Your Name, in godly fear and discipline, in virtue and obedience, that they may grow in purity of life and piety of faith, so that we may rejoice according to Your good pleasure, and praise You throughout our life. Through Jesus Christ our Lord. Amen.

Exorcisms

First Prayer of Exorcism by St Basil the Great

LET US PRAY TO THE LORD in the All-powerful Name of Jesus Christ. Lord, have mercy. O God of gods and Lord of lords, Creator of the fiery spirits, Maker of the fleshless powers, and Artificer of the invisible powers, Creator of all things heavenly and earthly: You Whom no man has seen -- nor is able to see; You Whom all creation fears and before Whom it trembles; You Who didst cast into the darkness of the abyss of Tartars the angels who did fall away with him who once was commander of the angelic host, who disobeyed You and pridefully refused to serve You, do You expel by the terror of Your name the evil one and his legions loose upon the earth, Lucifer and those with him who fell from above. Set him to flight and command him and his demons to depart completely. Let no harm come to them who are sealed in Your image and let those who are sealed receive dominion, "to tread on serpents and scorpions and all the power of the enemy." This we ask in the all-powerful Name of Jesus Christ. For You do we hymn and magnify and with every breath do we glorify Your All-Holy Name of the Father and of the Son and of the Holy Spirit, both now and forever. Amen.

Second Prayer of Exorcism by St Basil the Great

In the Name of Jesus Christ: I exorcize you, the beginner of sin and blasphemy, the leader of rebellion and worker of evil! I exorcize you who was thrown out from the light-bearing heights and was cast down into the darkness of the abyss because of arrogance. I exorcize you and all the fallen powers that follow your own design! I exorcize you, unclean spirit, by God Sabaoth and by all the ranks of the angels of God, Adonai, Elohi, Almighty God! Come out and depart from the servant of God in the Name of Jesus Christ!

In the Name of Jesus Christ: I exorcize you by God Who created all things through His Word and by our Lord Jesus Christ, His only-begotten Son, generated before all ages ineffably and dispassionately; Who created the visible and invisible creation and Who fashioned Man in His own Image; Who tutored him initially through natural means and Who protected him by the watchful care of the angels.

In the Name of Jesus Christ: I exorcize you by God, Who from on high flooded sin by water and Who opened the depths of heaven and destroyed the iniquitous giants and shook the tower of the ungodly and reduced the land of Sodom and Gomorrah to ashes by fire and brimstone and where the unending smoke is emitted as perpetual testimony; Who tore the sea asunder with a rod and led the people on dry land and Who destroyed in the waves of the water forever Pharaoh the tyrant and the God-fighting army and the enmity of ungodliness; Who in the last days became Incarnate ineffably from the pure Virgin and preserved intact the seals of purity; Who was pleased to wash away in baptism our ancient uncleanness which we had embraced by disobedience.

In the Name of Jesus Christ: I exorcize you by Jesus Christ! Who was baptized in the Jordan and had become a type of incorruptibility by grace in water and before Whom angels and all the powers of heaven stood astonished, beholding Incarnate God moderated, for the beginningless Father revealed the beginningless generation of he Son and the descent of the Holy Spirit testified to the unity of the Trinity.

In the Name of Jesus Christ: I exorcize you by Jesus Christ! Who rebuked the wind and calmed the waves of the sea; Who banished the array of demons and ordered the pupils of the eyes, missing from the womb, to be restored to sight by means of clay; Who renewed the ancient creation of our race and restored speech to the dumb and cleansed the sores of leprosy and raised the dead from the graves; Who held communion with man to the moment of the grave and Who by His rising destroyed hell, and Who made all humanity imperishable by His death.

In the Name of Jesus Christ: I exorcize you by God Pantocrator, the All-Powerful Sovereign Ruler! Who infused His Spirit into men by the

God-inspired voice and Who acted with the Apostles and filled the world with godliness.

In the Name of Jesus Christ: Fear! Flee! Be banished! Depart, unclean and abominable demon! Infernal, abysmal, deceptive, shapeless, visible because of your shamelessness, invisible because of your hypocrisy— wherever you have to leave or to exist or if you are the same Beelzebub, a demon that shakes, or one that is dragon-like, or one with a face of a beast, or one as vapor or appearing as smoke, or as a male or as a female, or as a creeping thing, or appearing as a fowl, or as one speaking by night, or one that is deaf or dumb, or as one that frightens by invasion or that convulses or attacks or exists in deep slumber or in sickness or in disease or rolling about in laughter, or inciting sensuous tears, or as a lewd spirit or foul smelling or covetous, or lustful, or sorcerous, or erotic, or horoscopic, or dwelling in a house, or one that is shameless, or contentious, or unstable, or changing according to the phases of the moon or one that flees at a certain time, or of the dawn or one instantaneously encountered, or if you were sent by someone or if you approached unawares, or one in the sea or in a stream or out of the earth or out of a well or a steep bank or a trench, or a lake or a reed orchard or out of matter or an unclean thing, or out of a forest or oak coppice or a tree or out of a bird or thunder or out of a bath chamber or out of a font of water or from a phantom tomb or from where we know not, either known or unknown, and from an unthought of place.

In the Name of Jesus Christ: Be divided and be removed! Be ashamed of the image created and fashioned by the hand of God! Fear the likeness of the Incarnate God and hide not in the servant of God (name)! For a rod of iron and a furnace of fire and Tartarus and the grinding of teeth and the recompense of disobedience await you.

In the Name of Jesus Christ: Do not return, neither hide with any other evil and unclean spirit! Rather, depart to the region which is waterless, desolate, uncultivated, and which no man inhabits and where God only watches over who binds all those that perpetrate the spell of the evil eye and assault His Image; Who with the chains of darkness banished to Tartarus to a long night and day, you, the Devil, the skillful worker and contriver of all evil! For great is the fear of God and great is the glory of the Father and of the Son and of the Holy Spirit. Amen.

Third Prayer of Exorcism by St Basil the Great

O God of Heaven! God of Lights! God of the angels that are under Your dominion, God of the archangels that are under Your power, God of the glorious principalities, God of the saints, the Father of our Lord Jesus Christ, You Who loosed the souls that were bound by death; Who by Your Only-Begotten Son illuminated humanity that was in darkness; You Who set us free from our pains and released us from every burden; Who kept every assault of the enemy away from us.

And You, Son and Logos of God, Who has made us immortal by Your death and has glorified us by Your own glory; Who by Your rising has granted humanity to advance to God; You Who by Your Cross carried every bond of our sins; Who took on and healed our offence; You Who put us on the way to Heaven, Lord, and changed corruption into incorruptibility:

Hearken to me as I cry out to You in desire and in fear! O Lord, before Whom the mountains melt from fright under the heavens and the firmament; before Whom the speechless souls of the elements shudder because of Your power, observing their own bounds; by Whom the fire of revenge does not exceed the bounds ordained for it but rather awaits Your will with groans; for Whom all creation travails, groaning in unutterable sighs and is ordered to await the seasons; from Whom all of nature flees away and through Whom the army of the enemy has been subdued and the Devil has fallen and the serpent trampled upon and the dragon is destroyed; through Whom the nations which confess You have been illuminated and in You have been made mighty, O Lord, through Whom life has appeared, hope is established, faith is made strong, the Gospel has been preached; through Whom no human has been refashioned from the earth, having believed upon You. For who is there like You, God Almighty?

Therefore, we pray to You, God of our fathers and Lord of mercy, eternal and superessential! Receive him/her who has come to You in Your Holy Name and that of Your beloved Child Jesus Christ, and of Your Holy and Almighty and Life-giving Spirit.

Expel from his/her soul every sickness, every unbelief, every unclean spirit that is convulsive, infernal, flaming, foul-smelling, covetous, greedy, avaricious, fornicating, tempestuous, every unclean demon that is dark, shapeless and shameless! Yes, God, take away from Your servant (name) every working of the Devil, all sorcery, witchcraft, drug addiction, idolatry, astrology, horoscopy, necromancy, ornescopy, divination, passion for pleasure, eros, avarice, wrath, contentiousness, instability, and every evil fancy.

Yes, Lord our God! Breath into him/her/them Your peaceful Spirit so that being protected by You, he/she/they might bring forth the fruit of faith, virtue, wisdom, purity, continence, love, kindness, a sound mind, prudence, for Your servant has called upon You in the Name of Jesus Christ, believing in the consubstantial Trinity, with the angels as witnesses, as well as the archangels and the glorious principalities and every heavenly host. Together, with him/her/them protect our own hearts, also, for You are mighty, O Lord, and to You we offer glory, to the Father and to the Son and to the Holy Spirit, now and forever. Amen.

Prayer for a Home Troubled by Evil Spirits

Let us pray to the Lord in the Holy Name of Jesus Christ. Lord have Mercy.

O Lord God of our salvation, Son of the Living God, Who is borne on the Cherubim, being above all dominions, principalities, authorities, and powers: You are great and fearsome to all around You. You are the One Who set the heavens like a vault and made the earth in Your might; Who directs the universe in Your wisdom. When earthquakes occur under heaven from the foundations, its pillars are unshaken. You speak and the sun does not shine. You sealed the stars. You forbid the seas and dried them up. Authorities and Dominions hid from Your wrath, and the rock trembles before You.

You obliterated the fates of brass and demolished the bars of iron. You bound the Mighty One and smashed his vessels. By Your Cross You cast down tyrants and drew the Serpent with the hook of Your humanity. And having cast him down, you bound him with hooks in the gloom of Tartary.

As the same Lord, the Hope of those who place their confirmation on You, and the Wall of might for those whose expectation is in You, (+) renounce, (+) drive away, (+) and transform all diabolical actions and all satanic indictments, (+) all slanders of the Adversary, and of the powers lying under this roof. Free those bearing the Sign which is awesome against demons—the Cross of Your Victory—and calling upon Your gracious Name from possession by him and from those wandering about under this roof.

Yes, Lord, You drove away legions of demons, and demons and unclean spirits by which the deaf and dumb were held. These You commanded to depart and not to return again. You have consumed all the armies of our invisible enemies, and have made wise the faithful who have known you. For You said, "Behold, I give you power to trample underfoot snakes and scorpions and all the power of enemies."

(+) Preserve, O Master, all who live in this house from all harm and every temptation from below, delivering them from the fear of the feeble one and the arrows that fly by day, from things proceeding from the darkness and attacks by demons at midday. Let Your servants and Your children, delighting in Your help, and preserved by armies of angles, faithfully sing as with one accord: "The Lord is Helper to me and I will not be afraid; what can man do to me?" and again, "I will fear no evil, for You are with me."

You are my Confirmation, O God, Mighty Master, Prince of Peace, and Father of the age to come. Your Kingdom is an eternal Kingdom, and to You alone is the Kingdom, and the Power, and the Glory, with the Father and the Holy Spirit, both now and forever. Amen.